WHY NURSERY SCHOOLS?

By the same author

PART-TIME NURSERY EDUCATION (1963)

WHY NURSERY SCHOOLS?

"In as much as ye did it"
—or did it NOT

G. M. GOLDSWORTHY

With a foreword by
Lord Boyle of Handsworth

1971
COLIN SMYTHE
GERRARDS CROSS

MADE AND PRINTED IN GREAT BRITAIN BY
THE GARDEN CITY PRESS LIMITED
LETCHWORTH, HERTFORDSHIRE
SG6 1JS

CONTENTS

ACKNOWLEDGEMENTS

The poem by Rudyard Kipling on p. 92 is reprinted by kind permission of Mrs. George Bambridge and Macmillan & Co. Ltd., and is taken from "The Just-So Stories".

"Some children are . . ." by Jo Lensford Oslo is reprinted by kind permission of the National Conference of Christians & Jews, New York.

"Little boys in Church" is reprinted here by kind permission of the author Robert Coffin and the Macmillan Company, New York.

FOREWORD

I am very pleased to have the privilege of contributing a foreword to *Why Nursery Schools?* Mrs. Goldsworthy, as I well remember from my days at the Ministry of Education, was always a consistent and courageous champion of better pre-school provision, long before the Plowden Report brought this subject into greater prominence.

Mrs. Goldsworthy's writing reveals her understanding of modern educational theory, her deep social conscience, and her rejection of the extremes both of "permissivism" and of authoritarianism. She believes that the right educational policy is "to ensure that the pendulum swings in the middle, so that children grow into creative and imaginative adults with disciplined minds". Mrs. Goldsworthy is one of those who recognize most clearly that even the youngest children, as a friend of mine once put it, "have flashes of mature thought". Her basic *respect* for children, and her desire that they should be helped to journey through their school life "with pleasure and confidence", are apparent throughout the book.

There is much excellent practical sense in these chapters—for instance, the summary of the ways in which parents, especially mothers, can most usefully co-operate with teachers. For instance : "As a busy wife and mother you may find it difficult to spare the time to listen to your child when he wishes to talk and communicate his ideas, but try to do this as often as possible." Surely this is just about the best single piece of advice that could be given to any parent.

I think Mrs. Goldsworthy is right to feel more optimistic about the future of nursery education; and I have in mind, as she does, both the plans of Government and also the more positive reaction of Parliament. Like so many books on education, this one is yet another reminder of the extra resources the service still needs if we are to do justice to the potential abilities of all young children within our society. But it is also an impressive testimony to what education means in terms of a heightened quality of life, and to the mutual benefit which both grown-ups and children can gain "from sharing the wonder and excitement of the world".

EDWARD BOYLE

INTRODUCTION

In as much as Ye did it . . . or did it not

"Be alive to the under-fives", preaches a road safety slogan. This advice and warning becomes more and more necessary every day as road traffic increases. The physical safety of children is of paramount importance for there is no wealth but life, but children are more than just physical beings with a digestive system. They have minds and spirits which must be nurtured from the very beginning if they are to grow into happy, honest, intelligent and co-operative citizens of tomorrow. "To make children capable of honesty is the beginning of education", said John Ruskin and this is one of the many aspects of character training promoted in good nursery schools and classes.

Nursery schools are not a wayside concession to charity. The education provided is not built on sand, even if the children sometimes play with sand. The foundations are not loose and shifting —they are deep and solid and sound.

Unfortunately, there is a section of the community, which includes some politicians and fanatically intellectual people, who tend to shrug their shoulders at any suggestion that nursery schools have more to commend them than some of the cheaper substitutes which provide good "minding". One reason for this attitude may be that they are unaware, or have forgotten, that there is such a thing as *skilled non-intervention* as well as *skilled intervention*.

Such people may need to be reminded, too, that nursery school teachers who are concerned with the day-to-day growth of individuals cannot produce impressive schemes of work as can teachers in other branches of education where subjects are taught.

It is not always obvious to a layman how a particular specialist

has spent his time. There is a lesson to be learned from the following light-hearted but true story reported in a Parish magazine.

Some years ago an artist was asked to "touch up" a large painting which hung in a very old church in his district. When he
presented his bill, payment was refused as full details of the work
done were not specified. The next day the artist presented the
account, itemized as follows:

Embellishing Pontious Pilate and putting new ribbons in his hat	8/-
Putting a tail on the rooster of St. Paul and amending his comb	6/-
Regilding the left wing of the Angel Gabriel	8/-
Washing the High Priest's servants	8/-
Renewing Heaven; adjusting the stars and cleaning up the moon	7/-
Brightening up the flames of Hell; putting a new tail on the Devil; mending his hoof and doing several odd jobs for the dammed	14/-
Touching up purgatory and restoring lost souls	7/-
Mending the shirt of the Prodigal Son	3/-
Touching up Pharaoh's Daughter.	3/-

It would be well for the critics and doubters, who might tend
to think of nursery school teachers as people who stand about
while the children play, to discover a little more about their work.
If these teachers have been well trained, and they put into practice all that they have learned at their Training Colleges, they
could be more aptly described as psychic midwives.

In recent months, the two main political parties have promised,
as part of their pre-election propaganda, an extension of nursery
education. Two years ago "The National Campaign for Nursery
Education" lobbied Parliament bearing a petition with 100,000
signatures and requested the provision of the state nursery schools
promised in the Education Act 1944.

On May Day this year, hundreds of children and their parents,
led by Mrs. Renee Short, the President of the N.C.N.E., arrived
at the Central Hall, Westminster, to present bunches of flowers

to guests celebrating the centenary of the Education Act of 1870. Among the flowers was a message: "Don't forget the under-fives."

This book has been written at this opportune time, in an attempt to enlighten people who are unaware of the value of nursery schools and the education they provide—an education through which growing children can enjoy fun and laughter which is part of their birthright—and at the same time experience love, beauty, truth, justice tolerance and loyalty. Through such an education there is a fair chance that, as adults, these same children will bring to a democracy a constructive attitude towards living. This would be an attitude imbued not only with courage and faith but an attitude rich in promise.

The many stories, which illustrate aspects of the work and the reaction of children in differing situations, are absolutely true. They were recorded by me during the many very happy years when I was responsible to the L.C.C. for the setting up and the supervision of nursery schools and classes. These stories may interest and amuse but it is important to remember that each one of the stories is a window through which imaginative adults can look into the mind of the child concerned.

Two slogans have already been mentioned. The third and most important is: "Give us more nursery schools." If these are provided in sufficient numbers throughout the country, there is hope that the young citizens of tomorrow will be social, disciplined beings who appreciate what is right and what is wrong; what is good and what is evil.

Later they may grow into:

Men with clear minds, pure hearts, true faith and ready
          hands;
Men who possess opinions and a will
Men whom the spoils of office cannot buy,
Men who have honour, men who will not lie:
Tall men, sun-crowned men who live above the fog
In public duty and in private thinking.

O. W. Holmes

It used to be said that it took nine tailors to make a man. Present day knowledge of children makes it clear that it takes almost as many skilled and patient people to make the growing child a good citizen of tomorrow.

The most important of these people are : Mother, Father, a well trained teacher and last, but by no means least, an imaginative and generous Government, which will enable all L.E.A's throughout the country to provide the necessary nursery school provision for all who need it.

This would be one of the effective ways of substituting hope and promise in place of the doctrine of despair which stems from all the evil in the world at the present time. It would be well to ignore the doubters and to remember what Adele Stevenson said of Mrs. Roosevelt at her memorial service : "She would rather light a candle than curse the darkness and her glow warmed the world."

Many responsible people would be willing disciples of the method which has been described if they were not hesitant to take action because they fear the over-all cost of separate nursery school buildings. It is right that the question of priorities in allocating finance for educational projects should be given serious thought. However, it is well worth remembering that the few essential needs of growing children, as far as the physical environment is concerned, are :

Space
Light
Good heating and ventilation
An interesting garden and adequate outdoor playing space.

Elaborate buildings are not necessary; money need not be spent on special "features" and elaborate fittings. I am reminded of two modern nursery schools. In one, the staff were able to carry out all the essentials of good nursery education with little physical effort—no sudden modification of plans was ever needed. In the other school, which cost very much more to build, the staff were able to satisfy the minimum needs of the children through the use of much ingenuity and often at the expense of unnecessary

* *

physical effort. It may be that in the interests of the children, staff and the ultimate cost of buildings it will be deemed wise to insist that Architects, who are not in the employ of L.E.A's, should visit good established nursery schools before they start planning.

Again, little thought has been given, so far, to the possibility of using temporary buildings which could be transported from one housing estate to another, as the needs of both districts changed. Many such buildings built in teak or a similar wood, are used in some Continental countries. They are both adequate and attractive.

In the meantime, while waiting hopefully for the promised plans to materialize, the optimists and the visionaries will continue to remember that the heart of a child is still soft and it must not be hardened or impoverished. If any hinder or cancel the promised plans their epitaphs could surely be :

"In as much as ye did it . . . *not*."

WHY NURSERY SCHOOLS ?

Sir George Newman in one of his annual reports said: "Let me make clear, precise and definite these facts:

1. That the child under five years stands at the gateway of our educational system.
2. That the child under five is the seed plot for everything medical, physical and moral.
3. That what happens to the child before he is five is bound, inevitably, to have results for good or evil."

The child under five stands at the gateway. All over the country there is a multitude of such children and their parents who are waiting longingly for the gates to be opened. Why have the gates been locked for so long? Unfortunately, for some time it has been politically expedient to hide the keys. Although the comparatively few existing nursery schools in this country have more than proved their worth, money was needed for other schemes. Some of these were connected with education but far removed from the important aspect of giving growing children the right start in life—giving them, in addition to the happiness which is their birthright, an opportunity to develop the qualities, abilities and aptitudes which would help them to become, later, acceptable members of the democracy of which we speak with such pride.

Financial priority has been given to higher education; to the extension of the school leaving age and to further education. Interest has been shown in scientific and technical education. As more becomes known of the preventive work of nursery schools and their ability to set standards and to offer wider horizons, it may be that more and more people will say with Professor Dewey: "I have never been able to feel much optimism regarding the possibilities of higher education when it is built upon such warped and weak foundations." The good builder of houses gives his thought and time first to the planning of good foundations and later concentrates on the roof and the balconies.

Unfortunately, I have no date on a report of a debate on Education which once took place in the House of Commons, during which Mr. W. Compton Carr, M.P. for Barons Court, made a plea for more nursery schools. Among other things he said: "I know that the reason very often given is that there is not enough money. It is a matter of priority but if I came to a choice—and I hope no one will take umbrage at this—between adults learning Russian at a few shillings a session, or indeed people learning scooter maintenance at a few shillings a session, I would have nursery education." I do not know Mr. Compton Carr but it is to be hoped that the House of Commons will soon be filled with M.P's who share his views.

When Miss Jennie Lee, as Art Minister, opened a College of Further Education at Hitchin she said: "If you have a young generation full of the joys of spring it will depend to a very great extent on the community *they grew up in* whether that vitality will enrich their lives or become destructive." What a responsibility this places on Governments, parents and teachers.

It is encouraging that there has been the sound of jingling keys in the House of Commons recently. We are assured that tentative plans are being made to extend nursery education. Perhaps it has been realized at last that the existence of our present modern sick society; the rebellious and aggressive attitude of many young adults; the heart breaking results of a destructive, rather than a constructive attitude to life might have been avoided had these anti-socials been given the opportunity, during their formative years, of enjoying joyous days while being prepared, skilfully but unobtrusively, for life as it should be lived in a democracy. Whatever the reasons for a commendable change of heart on the part of the Establishment, this is surely the time to emphasize the needs of a modern child and the ways in which good nursery education can satisfy those needs.

"A thousand mile journey begins with the first step" says an old Chinese proverb. Good nursery education helps a child to take his first firm step in the journey through his school life with pleasure and confidence and so prepare him for the world. It is important that the keys should not open the gates just because some misguided adults (educationists among them) feel that nursery education is a good preparation for the infants' school although it is true that the child who has benefited from such opportunities passes on to the next stage ready and eager to accept the challenge of learning the skills of reading, writing and number. This fact alone would make nursery education worth while but, what is more important is the fact that as he progresses through successive stages he does so with confidence and optimism. There has been a growing realization among Psychologists and Educationists, generally, concerning the importance of transitions in education. With skill and care these transitions can be a time of happy anticipation and ready adjustment. In the same way, the co-operation of parents and teachers can ensure that the transition from home to nursery school does not provoke strain or anxiety.

The many ways in which growing children can benefit from the educational opportunities provided through good nursery schools are dealt with in succeeding chapters. At this point it is necessary to draw attention to the miserable existence which many of them lead before the gates are opened to a better life.

The pioneers of nursery schools were concerned to remedy a social evil. The children of those far off days needed shelter, good food, fresh air, baths, rest and medical attention, as a means of promoting good *physical* health. These, together with a loving understanding which led to a sense of security, were provided in abundance by those saintly women of vision and sensitivity.

Today it is the exception, rather than the rule, to see children who are neglected physically but a wise and imaginative society must realize that a child is more than an animal with a digestive system; with limbs which must be exercised and with physical needs which must be satisfied to the exclusion of all else. He needs also the vitamins of *mental* health and for thousands of children today these are not available. Modern housing conditions are responsible to some extent for this.

Come with me in imagination for a walk through a modern

housing estate when children of compulsory school age are at their appropriate schools. Cast your eye from the bottom to the top of the many tall blocks of flats which are the pride and joy of so many architects and housing authorities—flats which are designed, first and foremost, to save ground space and then satisfy the constantly changing needs of the *adults* of this modern world. Seldom are the needs of the growing children given a thought.

As you look at this tall block of flats you will probably see at varying heights hands drawing aside window curtains and then the anxious eyes of a mother looking down to the hard, black, grim asphalt space below. Why is the gaze of each mother so anxious? Why do they peer from right to left? Nine times out of ten these mothers are making certain that their young children are safe; that they have not wandered into the nearby streets.

Let us leave this housing district and take a bus or tube to a different type of district, where parents with young children have been forced to live in expensive furnished rooms. The picture has changed. No longer will you see young children playing aimlessly on barren squares of asphalt. Instead, you will probably see over-dressed children whose hands are clutched by those of their mothers hurrying along the pavements.

Where are they going? Each mother, tired of coping with the impossible task of trying to keep a healthy, active child quiet and motionless, so that the landlord will not be disturbed or irritated, has decided to take the line of least resistance. So the time is spent walking the streets in the shopping areas or pushing through crowded chain stores. The child is lonely for he lacks companion-ship; the mother's mind is occupied with the many jobs she could be doing at home.

Is a visit to a chain store an exciting expedition for a very young child? Few of the goods for sale are on the child's eye level; he sees only trousered and skirted legs and, worse still, when the weather is wet he is also on a level with hundreds of dripping umbrellas. You will agree that this is a dreary picture of child-hood but it is one which is repeated thousands of times in every large city. One three-year-old child was heard to say as he

trundled round a large store : "Mummy, everything is *very* wet
down here."

Let me take you to another area where very small houses are
occupied by two families—on the ground and first floor. There
is one such area not very far from where I live. A local doctor
once said to me : "For God's sake try and persuade the head of
that infants' school to admit the Brown twins into her nursery
class; they have been on the waiting list for months." I explained
the difficulties facing heads in dealing with waiting lists but he
replied impatiently : "But this young mother is twenty-eight years
old but *physically* she is seventy."

I visited this home myself and was horrified to find two healthy
twin boys of three and a half years tied into chairs while the
mother finished some laundry and prepared the midday meal for
her husband.

The tenants living in the flat below were elderly and unable
to stand the noise of two healthy, vigorous children running from
one small room to the other. They expressed their annoyance by
banging on the ceilings with a broom. The young mother tried
to minimize the frequency of these reminders by tying her children into chairs until she was free to take them out. Eventually,
the twins were admitted to a nursery class where the teacher
provided the necessary scope for thir physical energy and the right
challenge for their stage of mental development. After two
months the improvement in the health of the mother and the
twins was impressive.

Before our tour ends, let us visit a residential area where blocks
of luxury flats are occupied by parents with high incomes.
Luxurious for the parents perhaps, but life in them can be mere
existence for the pre-school child. Often he is an "only" child
and surrounded by expensive toys of all kinds but he is lonely and
cut off (except on rare occasions) from the joy and excitement of
sharing experiences with his contemporaries. Furthermore, there
is a risk that these children suffer emotional stress as their parents
demand standards of behaviour which are to high.

What is the answer to this problem? Local Councils will point
with pride to the playgrounds often provided near their housing

estates and found frequently in parks. These are playgrounds where large fixed equipment provides little more than momentary pleasure for children who are at an age when they are longing to create, investigate and explore.

And what of the mothers who stand watching while their children play in this aimless fashion? They can be seen constantly referring to their wrist watches, for many of them have much to do in preparation for the return of older children and their fathers.

And what of the *many* days and weeks when, in our climate, the weather makes such an interlude impossible?

Many people reading this will say: "What about the *play groups* which are now being given so much publicity?" These, of course, are very much better than nothing but, except for a minority of them, the staff are untrained and little more than recreative play in a safe place is provided. The children are developing socially in such conditions; they can play happily with their contemporaries. This is far better than nothing at all but in no way must they be confused with nursery schools—where children are helped to develop mentally and spiritually, as well as socially. Furthermore, these play groups are few and far between and are seldom to be found in some of the areas where the need is greatest.

Other members of the public refer to day nurseries as a possible solution. These, of course, provide a *social service* and cater, generally, for the needs of unmarried mothers; widows; deserted mothers and so on, who are the only wage earners. These day nurseries are under the supervision of the Public Health Department and *of necessity* the days have to be very long with staff working on a shift system. They therefore tend to become a *substitute* for the home and not a *complement* to the home, as is the nursery school.

The solution is the provision of good nursery schools, with good well trained staff. Given this, children in a healthy, rich and colourful environment, where the right challenge and progression are provided for the individual, can develop qualities, abilities and attitudes which, not only make them eager and ready to make the most of what the next stage in education has to offer but, far more important, prepares them for life.

Many people who have a sincere interest in the welfare of children lift their hands in horror at the thought of parting them from their mothers, if only for two and a half hours. Much has been written in recent years about the effect of maternal deprivation on young children. The mother is, of course, the FOCUS of the young child's life and the importance of her role should never be under-estimated. What did the Prophet Buddha say?

> Who is the richest person here below?
> I would call the child with a loving mother rich.
> The child without a loving mother I would call poor :
> When one has a loving mother I would call it DAY
> When one has not a loving mother I would call it the setting of the sun.

A good loving mother realizes that it is one of her tasks to provide a bridge for her child—a bridge between his home and the vast outside world. The nursery school provides a stout, safe bridge.

One of my first questions when interviewing newly trained teachers was "Do you believe in parents?" A necessary question as close co-operation between staff and parents is absolutely essential if the child is to feel secure and happy. The gradual weaning from home to school encourages the child to look upon his stay there as a privilege, rather than an act of abandonment on the part of his mother. The good nursery school is a complement to the home and never a substitute for it. Furthermore, it is a medium of adult education for it can give much help to the uninformed or misinformed or over-anxious mother.

It is sometimes necessary however, to remind teachers, who are conscious of the mother child relationship, that care must be taken not to make too great a demand on the mother's time. Important as the child of nursery years may be, she has also a duty concerning preparations for the rest of her family and her husband.

Fairly often the situation is in reverse where the teacher has to help the mother give up her child. I have heard on many occasions "Why don't you go home now Mummy? I'll tell you all about it when you come to fetch me". Such a mother should be encouraged to leave.

Modern trends in nursery education have led to the establishment of many part-time nursery schools and nursery classes, when the children leave their homes for only two and a half hours in the morning or afternoon. From my own experience I know that such an arrangement can be successful in areas where the social background of the children is good. Part-time schools and classes have one disadvantage in that recruitment is limited to children living in the immediate neighbourhood. When the experimental part-time nursery education was started in London in 1953 there was, after a short time, a drastic "turnover" of children, as many parents who travelled by bus found it burdensome to make four journeys for a two and a half hour session. The advantages and disadvantages are dealt with in a later chapter.

The trained teacher

Next to the mother, the nursery teacher is perhaps the most important person to the child. It is reported that Michael Angelo was once heard muttering to a block of marble: "Within you lies both good and evil; what comes forth depends on me." What part does a good nursery teacher play in helping to bring out the inherent goodness in children?

Her part in the school day might appear to be a largely passive one for it is her role to observe and to guide, not to instruct. One of her most difficult tasks is so to efface herself that everything which a child can do for himself he is encouraged to do. She must be so sensitive to a child's every need that she recognizes when she can offer help and the most tactful way in which to offer it and—more often—when to withhold any suggestion of interference. The teacher must know when it is best to leave a child to overcome his difficulties alone so that he may win a sense of achievement, for her training and experience should tell her the capabilities of children at different stages of development. She must be quick to offer the right challenge at the right moment so that he does not become bored with fruitless repetition of effort. She must be capable of directing pugnacious tendencies into other channels so that they develop later into a gift of leadership of the right kind. She must be capable of satisfying the child's longing for love without making him dependent and she must recognize the very fine difference between licence and true liberty. The teacher is courteous at all times for "the grace of God lies in courtesy". She should have not only a sense of humour but an understanding of a child's sense of fun. This is an ideal to which only exceptional teachers attain but one which every good nursery teacher keeps before her.

She remembers too that, at this stage, the normal child spends his day in a continual search after truth. The following list of questions posed by an intelligent four-year-old during the course of a nursery school day illustrates this point:

What is eternity?
What is a waffle?
How do birds know where to go in the winter?
What makes winter come?
Why does Tuesday come after Monday?
Why do people die?
Where do they go when they *do* die?
If we must be kind to animals why do butchers kill sheep and
    cows?

Such provocative questions may provide a clue to the interests, and sometimes to the anxieties, of the questioner but they also provide evidence that the child is searching after truth. The search does not begin and end with asking adults to answer questions. All the child's activities which involve investigation, experiment or creative effort are a continuation of this all important quest. "Why?" "When?" "Why not?" "It should." "Fancy that!" "That isn't quite right." Such are the questions and comments that accompany the search. To make this search after truth a satisfying one the good nursery school or class provides an environment rich in opportunity, and purposeful activity is guided unobtrusively into the right channels. This is one of the most important functions of nursery education.

The pattern of the day

This should provide a rhythm of activity and repose which is essential to the promotion of good psychological as well as physical health.

After a personal greeting, which assures the child that he is an individual and not just a name on a register, every child occupies himself with material of his own choosing. The rich, colourful environment has been carefully prepared in every detail and it provides a stimulus to action. The importance of the long, uninterrupted play period which follows cannot be over-estimated, for it is not a pastime or a means of recreation. This so-called play is the greatest psychological need of the child. In the words of Froebel, "it begets joy, freedom, contentment, repose within and without and peace with the world". Through this purposeful play :

children develop confidence, control and skills of all kinds, including manipulative skill;
they develop self-reliance, patience and persistence—all good character training;
they develop *intellectually* because they learn to reason and compare;
they develop emotionally, for many opportunities, particularly those for fantasy play, allow them to identify themselves with other people.
Such opportunities provide an outlet for feelings of tenderness, sorrow, aggression, joy and frustration.

It is at this time too that children develop the ability to concentrate. Where children are given such opportunities, it is unlikely that parents will receive at later stages in our educational system the kind of report which includes such phrases as, "He is incapable of making a sustained effort", or "He is afraid to express himself fully".

The growth of children is, of course, gradual; the rate of

growth differs with every child; a true and full appreciation of this fact is essential if progress is to be satisfactory, for

> Seeds are not fruit nor are buds blossoms, but only promises
>   which flower or wither in their growing.
> Likewise a child is a child and not an adult . . .
> A child is a body shaping to health and competence,
> A mind tempering to thought and understanding,
> A soul fashioning to beauty and truth.

To meet the need for a rhythm of activity and repose, the play period is often followed by a quiet time for informal conversation, for stories and simple thanksgiving. The ability to communicate through speech is a uniquely human quality and opportunity to do this is essential. Moreover, difficulty in expressing himself through speech may lead to a child finding difficulty in learning to read. So the good teacher is never too busy to listen. Standing at a bus-stop one day, I heard one child say to another: "Have you got a Granny?" When she was told that there was no Grannie in the family the reply was: "I should see about getting one if you can because Grannies always have plenty of time to listen."

The happy time given every day to story telling helps to increase the child's vocabulary and to widen his knowledge of the world. Listening to suitable, well told stories and the provision of a variety of suitable books make it possible to share with children a small part of our great literary heritage.

In addition to these periods of quiet group activities, the need of an individual child for moments alone, away from a group in a screened corner, are respected. These are moments when a child can ponder on the thoughts which are his and can never be ours.

A short time devoted to music ensures that children are introduced gradually to a wealth of folk lore. Music is part of the cultural heritage of childhood so movement to music, interpreting it in their own way; listening to music (and this need not be limited to nursery rhymes and jingles); and singing provide valuable creative experiences and occasionally a relief from tension.

So, let the sound of jingling keys be replaced by the click of opening locks so that that the gates can be flung open and the citizens of the future can skip into a world where social, intellectual, as well as physical growth is promoted.

As *WE* perceive dully or clearly
As *WE* think fuzzily or sharply
As *WE* believe foolishly or wisely
As *WE* dream drably or goldenly
As *WE* bear false witness or tell the truth

THUS A CHILD LEARNS

PLAY—

The greatest psychological need of the growing child

"Psychological studies of 'Play' have revealed that this self-motivated activity of children, if provided under really good conditions, is productive not only of mental vigour, shown in thinking and reasoning, but also of much learning through the acquisition of rich experiences. Moreover, it is of value to the child's emotional satisfaction and stability allowing him to externalize his feelings in dramatic and artistic expression and to share them with others. The deep satisfaction of creative achievement gives a motive for self-discipline and self-control and it is evident that co-operation can reach its highest level in the medium of play."

This is one of the opening paragraphs in a memorandum of evidence sent to the Central Advisory Council for Education, under the Chairmanship of Lady Plowden.

By the time a normal child is old enough to enter a nursery school or class he has left far behind him the stage where he enjoyed rattles, large coloured beads or strings dangling from the hood of his pram, or the empty saucepans with varying sized lids and other improvized playthings provided by the imaginative mother to interest him while in his playpen. A large number of intelligent children have also lost some of their interest in the pushing and pulling toys which probably satisfied them from the age of approximately two years. So much depends on the facilities for unrestricted movements in the home. The flat in a large block and the small house without a garden fail to provide the necessary space for this stage in development, when the child is an egoist and has little interest in being one of a group. For this reason, a limited number of such toys may be made available in the nursery school so that the children who have been deprived of this experience can be satisfied, before they pass on to the next stage.

Most of the equipment in the good nursery school stimulates play which is not purely recreative but also provides a learning experience, if shared with contemporaries. Play then becomes, also, a joyous manifestation of developing personality.

For some time there has been much concentration on Scientific and Technical Education but certain aspects of our present society provide unmistakable evidence that we need not only better thinkers, better scientists and technicians, and vigorous creative people but better *co-operators*, too.

If a growing child plays happily it is almost always a sign that he is mentally healthy; on the other hand if he does not know how to play it is a sure sign that he is mentally sick. It was Dr. Montessori, the Italian educationist, who said: "There is a hidden MAN, a hidden child; a buried being who must be liberated. Here is the first urgent task of education. Liberation in this sense means knowledge, or indeed, a discovery of the unknown." Although the apparatus designed by Dr. Montessori and demonstrated by her are considered by many to be too limited for the average modern child, she must have had undoubted success in liberating the children of her country in those days, for when Mussolini came to power he closed down all the nursery schools. Was he afraid, one wonders, that the liberation of children might lead, later, to a hindrance in the processes involved in establishing a Dictatorship?

The young of every species spend their earliest days in play. If we consider the play of animals it is obvious that their "play" prepares them for their life as adults. When a kitten plays with a reel, rolling on it and then springing on it, as his mother does with a mouse, he is training his eyes and muscles for an important need of his adult life. Otters make slides for their young; clever photographs have given us wonderful illustrations of Dolphins at play and the antics of young seals on Seal Island. Compare this with the lamb which skips about for a very short time and all too soon adopts the habits of the solid sheep, or the colt which staggers on to its feet immediately it is born and is soon running around the field.

Monkeys and apes, which are nearest to humans, play in various ways right on to maturity. The research done by a well-known scientific biologist proves that curiosity, attention and memory play a great part in the education of young animals through their play, and that those species which are able to *learn* more *play* more—and for a longer period. No babies play for as long a period as human children.

When the human baby is born he has no power to observe objects. He is capable only of a few random movements, like stretching and a few reflexes like sucking and crying. Gradual progress in holding and clutching; making sounds which later become words; learning to crawl and walk. Then he is ready to jump, skip, throw, climb and balance, and he repeats these movements endlessly to develop his strength and skill. All types of play at every stage have a deep significance.

Froebel said: "For the child, play begets joy, freedom, contentment, repose within and without and peace with the world." In saying this, Froebel crystallized what research workers were beginning to know. Observation of children has proved that, through the wide variety of play experience provided in nursery schools, they can strengthen and develop their bodies; learn control and skills; learn to reason and compare; to think and to discriminate and to use imagination. While doing all this the ability to concentrate is being developed and so follows the beginning of intellectual reasoning.

Realizing this let us remember again the "deprived" children who have little but overcrowded homes and the sordid streets of the immediate neighbourhood to stimulate imagination; and the children from some very prosperous homes, whose chief excitement consists of travelling in fast cars or taking sedate walks or playing alone with unsuitable expensive toys.

Fortunately, there is another group of parents who, realizing all that their children are missing, do their utmost to spare time to enable them to enjoy any opportunities for recreative play which may be provided in the neighbourhood by Local Councils.

These wise people wait anxiously for an extension of real nursery education, when the tactful supervision and guidance of teachers trained in child development will ensure progression and challenge, in addition to happy recreation.

A visitor to a good nursery school will see a simple, well-designed, one-storied building set in an easily supervised garden. This garden provides not only areas of grass on different levels but flower beds, bushes and trees. These arouse in the children a sense of wonder and of beauty as season succeeds season; while the bird bath and feeding table and all animals, such as rabbits, hamsters and guinea pigs kept in hutches, will teach them much about the cycle of life and arouse in them feelings of tenderness and compassion. The keeping of pets may also provide an opportunity for answering simply and truthfully questions on sex.

Well made winding paths provide the opportunity for learning to ride and steer or to run or skip, while the large sandpit on the main section of the playground not only produces great physical energy but incites experiment and encourages ingenuity. Large fixed equipment for climbing, sliding and balancing provide an outlet for boundless physical energy while aiding physical growth. Children are helped to become confident and foot-sure and release from any kind of emotional stress is found in ways which will not upset adults. Such play also refreshes children after a period of concentrated effort on creative experience.

From the spacious, well-ventilated playrooms with low windows, access to the garden is direct. In these playrooms the visitor would see children absorbed in using creative materials such as clay, dough and paint. The creative work of children, when using long-handled brushes and a variety of coloured paints as they work on large sheets of paper fastened to low easels, has astounded many people in recent years. What must be remembered, too, is that a child may use this medium to "talk" to adults and to express apprehension or fear. For instance, a four-year-old girl painted excitedly for many weeks, always using the brightest colours. Quite suddenly she used only black and deep purple. Her teacher discovered that the child's mother was seriously ill and had been rushed off to hospital. All the time she was away the bright colours were ignored but one morning she rushed to an easel, plunged her brushes into pots of red and blue and green paint and there was a riot of colour on her paper. Her mother had recovered and was due home that evening.

Water, "which is very serviceable unto us and is humble precious and clean", is provided in good-sized tanks with suitable measuring mugs; syphons and strainers to encourage experiment and increase knowledge.

Pastry making is a popular choice of occupation and the children learn much from weighing and measuring the appropriate ingredients, making the pastry and then cooking their tarts or cakes in the school kitchens. It will be seen that such an activity can lead to interesting conversation and to an extension of vocabulary. On one occasion I was accompanied by a visitor who watched with interest a group of children occupied in this way. She duly admired the large biscuits with cherries in the centre and she was told that the following day the same kind of biscuits would be made, but the cherries would be replaced by nuts. To the question : "Do you know what we shall have to do to these nuts?" she replied "I expect you will have to skin them." Neither of us was prepared for the remark : "The correct word is 'blanch'."

Sensory material which is self corrective gives children an opportunity to develop manipulative skill and challenges their ability to master materials and the use of tools. A woodwork bench with larger tools, graded according to the ability and age of the child using them, is another popular occupation. Some children will sit quietly for a time in the Book corner; others will develop discrimination while solving large, interesting puzzles, while some may be seen enjoying the nature table and gazing at items through large magnifying glasses.

At approximately four years of age normal children love identifying themselves with other people and to satisfy this need a "home" corner suitably furnished and with "dressing up" clothes near at hand is provided. Elsewhere I have recounted stories which illustrate the ability of children to identify themselves with their parents but their powers do not end there. Their general observation of people outside the home may result in them turning themselves into teachers; doctors; bus conductors; builders; decorators and so on. There was a day when I was invited to join a queue of children standing near a screen behind which a "doctor" and some "nurses" were dressed appropriately. After my interview with the "doctor", when a miniature stethoscope was placed on my chest, I was handed over to one of the nurses who scribbled on a pad. As she gave me the piece of paper she said, in a very business like way, "This says come back again tomorrow morning at eleven o'clock."

At another "hospital" I watched a five-year-old "doctor" place his stethoscope on the arms, legs and head of a "patient" but never on his chest. After about ten minutes, the "patient" jumped off the stretcher bed and strode away saying "You don't know how to use a stethoscope. *I've died three times already.*"

At another school a five-year-old girl invited me to join her at a table set out for tea. As I drank the imaginary beverage, she left me abruptly. When she re-appeared, I thought it an opportunity to give her a little social training, so I said calmly: "You know, Doris, when you invite a friend to have tea with you it is not good manners to leave her sitting alone!" The quick reply was: "Now don't be impatient, I just left you for a few minutes to fly over to Germany where they make the most delicious cream cakes," and she placed in the centre of the table a plate containing a variety of leaves.

It is far from easy to follow the workings of a child's mind when he is indulging in fantasy play. I once saw an intelligent girl making dots with a sharply pointed pencil all over the body of a large plastic doll. I suggested that she might ask the teacher for some paper, if she were anxious to try and write. Her reply? "I'm afraid you don't understand. This doll is going to have measles in a minute."

As children approach the age of five years they sometimes lose interest in fantasy play and prefer to make things with the help of wood, paper, glue and scissors and to shape more elaborate models in clay, extending the process to colouring, baking and varnishing them.

Whatever the type of play, they need freedom to move and to choose; they need access to small stores of junk material so that they can carry out any ideas or improvizations. This description of a nursery school may sound so attractive that the uninitiated observer might ask: What are the teachers doing while there is all this happy activity? They have been doing a great deal in an unobtrusive way. Not only have they provided a large choice of materials, and these may vary from day to day, but they are observing quietly and are ready to come forward when any child is in need of help or guidance, encouragement or restraint. They have to be imaginative and resourceful in providing extra or different material which may be needed by an individual child before he can finish working out his theories. The well trained teacher is keenly aware of every child:

What he is doing
What he did yesterday
What stage he might be at tomorrow.

She is ever ready to encourage or sypmathize, to explain or correct. The child who suddenly becomes aggressive is led tactfully to the woodwork bench, where he can work out his anger in a legitimate way, or he may be encouraged to work on a large lump of wet clay, where he can pinch or thump to his heart's content.

As recently as April 13th this year, a psychologist at Nottingham University stressed at a Southampton conference the connection between lack of suitable toys and aggression. He stated that children who enjoy playing with a variety of toys are less likely than others to copy the violence on TV or in films. This was put to the test and results showed that those children who had been playing with toys were shown a film of a boy playing peacefully but who ended up by kicking an inflatable figure of a clown. When the children returned to their own toys it was found that those who had played longest, before watching the film, did not imitate the aggressive behaviour, while children who had not played with toys before they saw the film imitated the aggressiveness.

I once watched a forceful, dominant child in a country school who, without resorting to real aggression, made a timid boy who was his nearest companion do exactly what *he* wanted. This continued throughout the period and I wondered if the teacher had noticed this situation. I need not have been concerned. It was a warm sunny morning and the teacher planned a period of outside play. With chalk she drew several cross-roads on the asphalt and then invited some of the children (including the aggressor) to turn themselves into cars, motor cycles and buses. The timid boy was then invited to be the traffic policeman standing at the cross-roads. Then followed an interesting game for the group while the timid child was given the experience of directing the others. The dominant boy was in the far from enjoyable position of obeying instantly the directions given by his friend.

Another aspect of the teacher's responsibility is the necessity to ensure every morning that everything in the school is dainty, clean and attractive. The quality of play varies according to the state of the equipment. If it is shabby or incomplete it is unlikely that it will be treated with respect—perfection in these respects will encourage appreciation and care. The daintiness and beauty of the general environment where attractively arranged flowers, growing plants and suitable pictures hang at the eye level of the children, is a part of the good teacher's plan to set standards for life.

> A child went forth every day
> And the first object he looked upon
> That object he became
> And that object became part of him for the day
> —or a certain part of the day
> —or for many years
> —or for stretching cycles of years.
>
> *Walt Whitman*

The play of children is their WORK, but it is work which should invite laughter and joyous satisfaction. An epitaph on a 200-year-old tombstone says:

If your nose is close to the grindstone
And you hold it there long enough,
In time you'll say there are no such things
As brooks that babble and birds that sing;
Just these three things will all your world compose
Just you; the grindstone and your poor old nose!

In this modern world so full of noise and bustle and much ugliness; so full of intrigue and competition and a clamouring for power: there is a real danger that adults can become so absorbed in the immediate that the real meaning of life escapes us.

It is within the nation's power to ensure that the growing children of today are enabled to appreciate beauty and enjoy periods of repose, while learning through doing in a carefully planned environment. Their formative years are short—the world of the future may demand even more from them than it does from the adults of today.

Then sing, ye birds, sing sing a joyous song!
And let the young lamb abound
As to the tabor's sound.
We in thought will join your throng
Ye that pipe and ye that play,
Ye that through your hearts today
Feel the gladness of the May.

THE GROWING CHILD'S INTEREST IN WORDS—SPEECH DEVELOPMENT

To be able to communicate thoughts and ideas and to recount experiences through speech is one of the things which makes us "divinely human". It makes the young of our species unique.

Yet, in the role of parent and teacher, adults are so close to children while this is happening that there is a risk that they might lose sight of the unbelievable wonder of it all.
It is well to remember that :

At the age of one year a child has a vocabulary of approximately three words.

At the age of two years this has increased to approximately twenty-nine words.

At the age of three years the child's vocabulary consists of approximately 272 words.

Is not this in itself a miracle? Remembering these facts, adults should think more than twice before requesting a child to stop talking. Only by listening to good speech and by talking himself can a child's vocabulary increase gradually but surely until, in an amazingly short time, he can express himself with clarity, sequence and a simple logic. Pondering on such things should make us adults feel very humble.

Recently I stood in a bus queue immediately behind two young mothers who chatted earnestly about the merits or otherwise of various soap powders on sale in the nearby supermarket. As a forced listener, I became amazed at the fervour with which the discussion proceeded and the futility of the arguments brought forward. I wondered what their two small children were discussing with equal earnestness. This is what I heard:

> First child: "Well then, can you tell me what brains look like?"

> Second child: "Yes, I can. You ask your Mum to buy some walnuts next time she goes to the greengrocer. Crack one open and look inside the shell. Then you will know what brains look like."

Which of the two conversations was the most interesting, enlightening and more indicative of intelligent thought?

A doctor writing in a Sunday newspaper expressed his irritation over the tendency of some mothers to talk to their young children as "woman to woman" or "woman to man". "They are only young once", he pleaded. He obviously delighted in the patronizing baby talk used by less intelligent mothers trying to make contact with their young.

What would this doctor have thought had he visited a nursery school in S.E. London at the time a teacher was showing a group of children a beautifully arranged bowl of flowers? "What do you think of these?" she asked. "I think they make a most pleasing sight" answered a five-year-old. Later on the same morning he would have been even more surprised. After moving spontaneously to music for some time the teacher asked the children to sit down and said: "Now while we are all having a rest we can listen to some lovely music." Turning to a pile of gramophone records, she murmured: "Now, I wonder which one they would like?" Immediately, a four-year-old called out: "Miss X, have you anything by Debussy by any chance?"

Why should a child have to re-learn words? Why not "good-bye," which is a corruption of "God be with you," rather than "Ta-ta"?

An intelligent three-year-old child who was well known to me, regularly spent the first few minutes of the afternoon rest time, in a full-day nursery school, lulling himself to sleep by repeating: "Quack, Quack? No, no, Malcolm, not Quack, Quack—Duck. Moo, Moo? No, no, Malcolm, not Moo, Moo—

Cow. Ba, Ba? No, no, Malcolm, not Ba, Ba—Sheep." When he had worked his way through all the farmyard animals he would end his soliloquy by saying: "Blood! Blood! Blood!" On the third "Blood" he was fast asleep.

Similarly, a nervous two and a half-year old always asked the nearest adult to repeat the word "potatoes" as he tried to woo sleep. If there was a pause in the monotonous repetition of this word he would open an eye and plead: "Go on!—say potatoes." When this was done for approximately five minutes he would give a deep sigh and fall asleep.

Children are capable of coining words which might make useful additions to our language. The boy who described his pet as "a most *barkative* dog"; the girl who reported her mother's illness by saying "she has an *influation* cough" and the description of a bulldozer removing wet sand from a river bed as "glooping up the mud" are examples of this.

A young father was asked by his four-year-old son son why the bus on which they were to travel had been stationary for such a long time. He replied: "I think there is probably some carburettor trouble just like we had with our car." The boy's comment was: "Don't be silly, Dad, buses don't have carburettors! They have busurettors."

A four-year-old boy in a nursery class in a Roman Catholic school told me that he and all his family were flying to Ireland for their holiday. I assured him that this would be a very interesting experience. His friend then told me that all his family were going to Ireland, too. To my question: "Are you going by aeroplane?" the immediate reply was: "Oh. No! We are going by taxi; train; boat and taxi."

One day, while waiting for the nursery class children in a N. London school to replace their socks and shoes after musical movement, I stood admiring the paintings on the classroom wall. I remarked to the teacher "They are lovely, especially that picture of a kangaroo." Suddenly, a firm hand was placed on my arm and I heard: "That is my picture and it is a giraffe, not a kangaroo."

I thought this was the end of the discussion but it was

not. As the teacher and the rest of the class walked quickly through the Hall to the main nursery classroom, I found myself walking with Audrey and the following conversation took place :

> Audrey : "Mrs. Goldsworthy, there are quite a number of things which you don't know anything about, aren't there ?"
>
> Reply : "Well, Audrey, there are so many things in this world that it would be impossible for me to know even a little bit about all of them, but what are you thinking about particularly?"
>
> Audrey : "Well, you don't seem to know the difference between a giraffe and a kangaroo, and you don't seem to know that the last person leaving a room always closes the door."
>
> Reply : "If I did not close the door I will go back and do so now."

When this was done Audrey squeezed my hand : gave me a lovely smile and we walked down the corridor talking of other things.

In giving growing children a wide background of experience and, while they are enjoying these experiences, helping them to express their ideas in sentences and with correct usage and, in addition, listening with genuine interest when they wish to recount their ideas and impressions the nursery school teacher builds a firm foundation in readiness for the time when they are physically and psychologically ready to learn the skill of reading. It is very unlikely that the four-year-olds I have just described, who were able to carry on a conversation with such social ease, found any difficulty in learning to read when they had the right degree of eye co-ordination to focus on a printed symbol and to see it clearly.

A teacher may not be a beauty by Hollywood standards but she can be the most wonderful person in the eyes of the three to five-year-olds. Not only do they tend to immitate the manners and mannerisms; accept her ideas and love what *she* finds lovely but they often acquire her vocabularly and the quality of her voice. If she gives them the opportunity to express themselves freely they will then advance towards a directness and logic which is impressive.

One day a four-year-old greeted me courteously as I entered a nursery school and then said: "Now *you* have got the time to explain to me simply and quickly the difference between a reflection and a shadow." The headmistress gave me the use of the small medical room. I blacked out the windows and, with the help of a torch and some mirrors, I did my best to satisfy the boy's thirst for knowledge.

When the demonstration ended, he thanked me and said: "You *have* explained the difference very simply—but not very quickly, I'm afraid." He then skipped away to find some other occupation to challenge his powers.

I found it difficult to believe, when he passed on the following information to me, that William, a Spanish boy in a N. London school, had arrived in England only six months before —unable to speak a word of English. "My fadder wanted to be a doctor so he came to England to train. He found a job and soon one of my fadder's friends he died so my fadder got his job, which was a better job. Then my fadder he sent for my brothers. Later on he sent for my mozzer and me so we all come to England. When I told someone zis story they say 'Well you come in dribs and drabs'. Tell me, please, what *are* dribs and drabs?"

It was at this school too that I was startled when a five-year-old asked me: "Mrs. Goldsworthy, what are your interests outside your work? Are you interested in archaeology by any chance?" I admitted that this subject bored me, to which she replied: "What a pity. If I had known that you were coming today I would have brought all my interesting pictures to show you. Never mind, let's go into the Hall and look at the skeleton which Mrs. X (the headmistress) has hung up for us all to see. Perhaps I can interest you in the human frame."

Unbelievable—but true!

By the time a child enters a nursery school or nursery class at the age of three years, he should have acquired a useful vocabulary—if his babyhood and early infancy have been normal. He may be retarded if his parents have not talked to him sufficiently or if their over indulgence in anticipating his every need has cut out the necessity for speech. If the incentive is removed the acquisition of speech is delayed.

It is often necessary for adults to explain the meaning of words and phrases which they use as part of ordinary speech. A lack of understanding can lead to confusion in the minds of children and sometimes to what adults might consider to be a lack of co-operation.

For instance, a mother who had been meticulous in following the advice of the teacher in visiting the school regularly, while her child was on the "waiting list", was more than a little perturbed when her daughter burst into tears at the end of her first short session. The following conversation took place when they reached home :

Child : "I don't want to go to that school again."

Mother : "What is the matter? You have always enjoyed visiting the school with me : you have a number of friends there and you know you like Miss X very much."

Child (sobbing) : "Miss X promised to give me a present and she never did."

After further chat the mother discovered that Miss X had said to the child on arrival : "Sit there *for the present*, dear."

Again, a teacher unknowingly confused a child by saying with a laugh : "I have green fingers." She gave this reply when he commented on the healthy state of the growing plants on the Nature Table. The next morning the boy arrived at school with his hands covered in green paint and announced : "I can look after all the plants now *and* make them grow."

Another day I was puzzled when I caught sight of a number of paintings depicting Cinderella, done by children of six years and over. Included in every picture was a large coloured ball. I heard later that a young teacher, when telling the story of

Cinderella, had omitted to explain that a Ball was the name given to a very special kind of dance.

On another occasion an adult questioned a child about a large black spot on his picture of Mary and the Christ child sitting on a donkey led by Joseph. His reply was: "That is the flea. You see, Joseph was told to take Mary and the Christ child and flea into Egypt." This child was also confused by the double meaning given to words.

The following story is heart-rending—in that it emphasizes the misery which a child can experience through ignorance of the meaning of words: misery which could have been avoided had the parents been more attentive to family conversation.

Whenever I visited a certain nursery class in N. London I had always been impressed by the intelligence and the joyous activity of a particular child. Imagine my surprise when, on a subsequent visit, I found her sitting unoccupied in a corner of the room looking listless and miserable. It was obvious that she had been crying. The teacher told me that she had been in this state for several weeks but she had no clue to the cause, except that the child often repeated the word: "Sums, sums". I settled down with Eileen and after a time I succeeded in interesting her in some new apparatus. We "played" together for over an hour, and then I said quite suddenly: "You must excuse me for a few minutes, Eileen, I want to do some sums." At the sound of this word the child became slightly hysterical and shouted: "No, not sums! *not sums.*" With my arm round her shoulders, I then proceeded to do a few very simple additions using coloured counters. After a few minutes, Eileen's face lit up in a way which I shall never forget. She almost shouted with relief as she called out: "Is *that* what sums are?" She then ran off, joined a group of children and proceeded to share their play activities.

Somewhat baffled, I investigated further when the mother arrived at the end of the day. I discovered that a brother in the junior school had been taunting Eileen every evening for several weeks saying: "You wait until you leave that nursery class and go up into the infants' school. Then you will have sums my girl, you'll have sums." As the child was due to enter the infants' school proper in a matter of a few weeks, her misery became more acute with each succeeding evening.

This section on the importance of encouraging the child's interest in words would not be complete without a record of a monologue by a five-year-old child in an American nursery school. His nursery school teacher, realizing that he was confused and troubled and seemed to be seeking comfort and relief from his emotional tension, arranged to sit at a table pretending to be absorbed in some reading, while the child talked to her. The school secretary sat near by and recorded everything which was said.

The reading of this monologue should leave no adult in doubt that as children develop in other ways they should be helped to increase their vocabulary so that their thoughts, whether happy or sad, can be expressed in words.

A Long Time to Wait—Monologue on Growing Up

by a five-year-old-boy

(Recorded in an American nursery school)

"Today I'm not gonna be big. I'm gonna be a little baby and you must take care of me. I can't do *anything* for myself. I can just lie in your lap. I'm tired of being a big boy for a while.

"It's awful the way you go on being big. Of course you want to grow big but you couldn't help it if you *didn't* want to. You just keep on growing. It would be awful if you didn't like it 'cause it would just go on anyhow and how sad that would be.

"But being big is the best, best thing, isn't it? When you're big everything happens, instead of just waiting to be big. When you get big you can do what you want to do and nobody tells you and you don't have to ask. You just go ahead and do what you want. And you can tell other people. That's a good thing.

"When I'm big I'm not going to be afraid of *anything* and I'm not going to cry *ever*! People who cry when they are big are silly. When my mommy cries she says it's because she loves sister and me and things make her sad. I guess I won't love anybody. I'll take care of mommy and sister but I won't love them enough to make me cry. I will be *very* big and strong and I'll kill a lot of people, and I'll take care of people if they want me to but still be all by myself.

"But not now. Today you must take care of me. Do you hear me? I am a little baby. Only don't tell anyone that. I wish you would pay attention to me instead of always writing. That's being big. You don't have to pay attention if you don't want to.

"It would be funny if I was big and you were little. I wouldn't pay any attention to you and I'd make you do things you didn't like to. But I guess I won't ever be able to do that to you 'cause I won't ever be able to catch up to you. I won't ever be able to be the same as you at the same time. It would be funny if when you were born you were grown up wouldn't it? And then instead of getting old you got younger and littler till you were a baby. That would be funny.

"What if that happened now? It would mix people up a lot wouldn't it? I wish you were a baby so I could take care of you.

"Do you know how babies come? They are part of the mother and father—sister told me. If you were my baby you would be part of me. I would take care of you and feed you and give you a bath and dress you and let you come in my bed and kiss you and not let anybody shoot you. I would kill all the people who came near. Killing people must be very easy because people aren't much. And they do a lot of it.

"On the other side of the ocean, if you were there, we might be dead now. Did you know that? It is not safe there. Not many places is safe. Even this place is not very safe. There may be shooting here some day too. I wish we could run away from it, but everywhere you go there is shooting. It makes me so afraid.

"It makes me dream and I wake up crying—being scared like that.

"Some day if I grow up and I guess I will, I'll have to shoot too. Sometimes I wish I didn't have to grow big. *NOW!* that's why you must take care of me and we will pretend I'm a little baby and have a long time to wait till I grow big. I wish you would. Are you listening to me?"

To end on a happier note, the following account of a holiday in France was told by Jimmy, aged four and three quarter years, who attended a Nursery class in N. London. At the beginning of each new term the teacher encouraged the children to talk about the holiday and how they had spent their time.

This is one of a collection of stories recounted by different children and recorded by the nursery assistant, who sat unobtrusively in a corner of the room.

My Holiday in France

"I went to the South of France by Comet and I came back on the Super Constellation. There was a cat called Pootsey and another cat called Tiger Tim at the house where I stayed, and a dog called 'Jilly', and I went to the beach a lot and I did the back-stroke every time I went into the sea. Every morning I went to meet the postman, except Sunday. He had lots of letters for everybody, some for me, some for Daddy and some for the people who lived round the back of the house.

"We had breakfast outside the house because there was a table outside, you see, and we sat out there for lunch, and always in the morning Jilly would sit on the bench.

"On one of the beaches I collected coloured glass. I left some in France and brought some back to Hamilton Terrace, where I live, and tomorrow I will bring some to school.

"Sometimes Mummy got me up in the night so that I

Concentration

Experimenting with water.

The Creative Urge

Simple Weaving: concentration while developing manipulative skill

could see the fireflies. They looked like flashing lights, and once Daddy got me up to see a toad just by the edge of lots of stones going down to one of the steps.

"The bathroom had different chains in, one for the lavatory, another for the sink, and in my bedroom there was a chain to save me washing in the bathroom.

"Before I went on the Super Constellation I got up and somebody in the house drove us to Nice, that is where the Airport is, and we got on the 'plane. We reached London just in time for breakfast, and that was the end of my holiday."

Jimmy was fortunate in having parents, who could not only give him such a wonderful opportunity to travel but, who were also sufficiently imaginative to enable him to see fireflies and toads. It is unlikely that Jimmy will grow into the kind of man described by Humbert Wolfe :

> The city financier walks in the garden
> Sadly because of his pride and his burdens.
> The daisies, looking up, observe
> Only a self-respecting curve;
> The thrushes only see a flat
> Tableland of shiny hat.
> He looks impatiently about him
> And all the Spring goes on without him.

FREEDOM AND THE LAWS OF
THE COMMUNITY

Everything that lives,
lives not alone or for itself

BLAKE

Sir Francis Mander once said: "The good school has now become a social community within which children no longer live to learn but learn to live. It embodies a way of life within which the ideas of unique personality on the one hand and the community basis of society on the other are in the process of being harmonized. The new outlook in education means that the main emphasis is on the whole child. The demand for the development of the personality of each individual child roots itself in a religious and a democratic soil."

In a nutshell, learning to live together should be more important than acquiring information, and the task of teachers is so to live with young children while they are teaching them that they fulfill their human possibilities. All adults in close touch with growing children have to play their part in preparing them for the responsibilities of active citizenship, remembering always that in order to be good citizens we must first be good men and good women.

The home is the first and most important place for this kind of training: it gives the first teaching. It is in the intimacy of his home that a child first feels a sense of security or insecurity; where he first realizes that he is loved or unloved respected as an individual or ignored as someone with no rights of any kind. The nursery school comes second to the home in this but it is important to remember that even the very many happy home backgrounds can differ in a very real sense. There is no strict formula for a happy home, whatever the class of society, except the need for love, patience, respect and understanding combined with a firm and stable system of human values.

Many social and personal attitudes are fixed before children enter a nursery school at the age of three years, but even if some of them are far from being good, the skilled teacher knows that there is no reason for despondency. There is something in the nature of a parable in a story which started one night during a London air raid. An old building received a direct hit and from one of the parapets there was thrown into a nearby garden a large piece of stone. It happened that the garden belonged to a sculptor and he later carved from that piece of stone what is considered to be his masterpiece.

So in the human debris which is occassionally tossed into our schools there is ready to hand opportunity for masterpieces of creative work. It is not possible to consider freedom in education without considering the need for legitimate discipline and the very fine line which exists between true freedom and licence. The growing child's need for control is basic and there is no more unfortunate misinterpretation than the idea that untutored licence is acceptable.

It is important to remember when considering discipline and freedom for children of this age that there must always be tolerance—tolerance of the mistakes made through lack of experience and tolerance of those mistakes which are the result of an unsuccessful effort to do the right thing.

Is it reasonable or fair to expect children who have been in the world for such a short time to be so near perfection that they are at all times controlled, reasonable and co-operative? How many of us have learned as much in other ways in a later period of five years in our respective lives? In the first five years we not only learned to :

feed—stretch—lift our heads
sit up—crawl—stand—balance
walk—run and climb

but we learned to **TALK** too. I have dealt elsewhere with this miracle of human speech by which we are able to *express* our own wishes and own thoughts.

It must be stressed that I have no sentimental or pretty picture of young children in my mind. During evacuation, when I lived all round the clock with up to one hundred children between the ages of three and five years, I learned more about children than I ever did during my years of experience before and after the war.

Children can be aggressive and anti-social; they can at times be so difficult that all our patience, tolerance and skill is demanded. Nevertheless it is important for adults to remember at all times that every child is a miracle of creation : "Every child comes with the message that God is not yet discouraged of man."

The good nursery school is a place in which the child's aggressive impulses can find acceptance, but he is helped to transform his temper into healthy self-assertion; his jealousy into stimulating competitiveness; his destruction into construction. It would help adults if they remembered that when young children are obstinate and aggressive they are calling out "Help me! Stop me doing this : I cannot help myself."

If, by the time they entered the next stage in education, some of those children who have been fortunate enough to attend a nursery school or nursery class have *not* learned *to share* with other children and to *co-operate* with adults, the staff concerned should hold up mirrors to look at their own reflections. It is possible that they will not be completely satisfied with what they see.

> What is the supreme happiness here below?
> It is listening to the song of a child
> As he goes down the road
> After having asked me the way.

He asks the way but he does not necessarily need to be taken all the way.

Many critics of nursery schools—and there are still far too many of them—are usually uninformed about the aims and the ideals of the system and tend to say: "Nursery schools? Nursery classes? These are places where the children are free to do *what* they like; *when* they like; *how* they like!" The answer to such a criticism must be: "If this has been seen to happen, it was a bad nursery school or nursery class."

It might be well worth while to consider the word "Discipline" and its derivation. It comes from the same root as the word "Disciple" so discipline is connected with *learning*. In the modern dictionary discipline is described as "the orderly conduct and action which results from training".

In his book, *Painting as a pastime* Churchill wrote: "As for the unfortunate people who can command everything they want; who can gratify every caprice and lay their hands on almost every object of desire—for them a new pleasure, a new excitement is nothing. In vain they rush around frantically from place to place trying to escape from avenging boredom by mere chatter and motion. For them, discipline in one form or another is the most hopeful path."

This reminds me of the story of the little girl who asked in tones of misery: "Is this another day when I have to do what *I* like all day long?"

A reasoned view of discipline is surely a child's willing submission to the example of adults whom she admires, rather than subordination to the will of tyrants.

If it is our task and our privilege to show children the road on which they are to travel, it is as well for us to consider the kind of world for which we should be preparing them. It has been said that anyone who is not a democrat by the age of five years will never be a real democrat. It is therefore important that in their formative years children should be helped to accept ideas and opinions, but they should be allowed occasionally to reject ideas and opinions as long as they do so courteously. What adults must realize and face courageously is that we have a definite function to perform while children are travelling along this road.

What is this function? It involves keeping a balance between control and freedom at every stage; limiting a child's freedom to protect him from his own weakness and inexperience, and yet giving him the greatest possible opportunity to ensure a normal development. This demands a very special kind of relationship.

What are children free to do in a nursery school? They are free to *create* but not to *destroy*; to investigate and to explore within certain limits remembering always that the rules of saftey and health must be obeyed without question. We are now well aware that growing children have potentialities for creation through all kinds of media. To quote Dr. Hughes, once chief inspector for the L.C.C.: "Creativeness is the choicest flower of child development; its buds appear universally in the stage of babyhood, but too often they wither away in the frosts of insecurity before they come into full bloom."

The environment provided in a good nursery school is rich in opportunity for creative effort, while offering an endless succession of free choice. This freedom to create leads to joy and the richer the opportunities for creative expression the deeper is the joy. Where there is laughter and happiness springing from the joy of creation, there is little time for anti-social behaviour. In another chapter I have stressed the fact that the difficult child is usually a *bored* child.

An incident springs to my mind which illustrates this point extremely well, I think. A young, newly trained teacher was trying to cope with a four-year-old boy who spent his time rushing round the room worrying other children. When the opportunity arose, I asked him if it would not be more fun if he found something exciting in one of the cupboards—something which a boy of four would love to do. His quick reply was: "I can tell you, there ain't nothing in them cupboards which a boy of four would like to do." I followed this up with a joke and said: "Come on Reg. We will go together and look through those cupboards." After our combined investigation, I had to say: "You were quite right Reg. There isn't anything in these cupboards for a boy of four." He shouted at me: "I told you, didn't I?" and then rushed into the garden, where he continued to be a nuisance!

A supply of suitable equipment was soon sent to that nursery class and the young teacher was enabled to carry out the work for which she had recently been trained. Progression in types of activity which lead to a sense of achievement is essential if boredom is to be avoided. The truth of this was emphasized when I saw a small boy standing alone in a school playground watching an aeroplane flying overhead. The rest of his class had followed the teacher into the classroom. While standing there the boy was approached by the schoolkeeper and for several minutes they were engrossed in exchanging information about the aeroplane—its name; the number of engines; the possible wing span and the skill of the pilot. At this point, an anxious teacher called out : "Please come in at once Tommy." The boy gave the schoolkeeper a look of thanks; shrugged his shoulders and said : "Ah well! I suppose I must go in now and *thread a few beads.*"

Another function of the teacher when considering discipline and freedom is to remember that, in addition to the need for opportunity to *learn through doing,* there must also be opportunity for leisure. In recent years the stress placed on *activity, activity* and more *activity* tends to make the most responsible people forget or minimize the need for leisure, which has been aptly described as "floor space in an overcrowded room". The over-tired or over-stimulated child can quite easily become the undisciplined child.

I am saddened by the story of one such child who, when asked what she would like for her birthday, replied fervently: "I would love a bit of peace and quiet."

Every form of training requires its own discipline and, even in the freedom of the nursery school, discipline must involve a certain number of inflexible rules. Rules of safety and of health must be made and it is comforting to remind ourselves that children expect adults to provide these safeguards. If rules are kept to a minimum and the reason for them is explained and if there is always consistency in applying them the average child does not resent or resist. On all occasions in the home and at school nagging has little effect. The father who, when he returned home from work and expressed his surprise and disappointment because his small daughter looked so miserable, was told: "It's all right for you Daddy. You haven't been nagged by Mummy all day."

Tone of voice is all important in demanding obedience or co-operation. A gentle but firm tone is much more likely to have the desired effect than a harassed shout.

Part of the nursery school child's training for life in a democracy includes the teacher's insistence that he must think of the needs of the greater number. For instance, he is not forced to join in musical movement or in listening to stories but he *is* expected to occupy himself quietly in a corner of the room, while his contemporaries enjoy these opportunities. Incidentally, if children are expected to do this rather than be allowed to race around the garden at such a time, his recognition of the pleasure he is missing will encourage him to join the group on a subsequent occasion. After all a child cannot ask for marmalade if he has never tasted marmalade!

Aggression is stopped and it always has the desired effect, because if anyone fails at *anything* time after time and there is no hope of succeeding the effort ends.

For all ages and all sorts and all conditions of people, discipline is bound up with a sense of security. The child who becomes a bully first realizes the power of physical force when he uses it to prevent something being taken from him. An adult who resorts to corporal punishment for children of this age uses it most often when there is danger of adult authority being snatched away. In short, it is an admission of defeat.

Sir Norman Angel has spent much of his life trying to show the futility of war to the world. A five-year-old boy once summed up in one sentence the principles which Sir Norman had been trying to teach the nations. Walking along a corridor in a large infants' school, I came across a friendly schoolkeeper who was well known to me. He was talking firmly to a small boy and I heard him say: "Your Mummy has told me that you are always pinching your baby. Now, if I hear that you have done this again I am going to pinch you." Quietly and courteously the boy said: "And will you tell me who is going to pinch *you* for pinching *me*?"

Corporal punishment is not used in the good nursery school. If a child continues to be anti-social after every effort has been made to direct his energies into other channels, he is isolated from the group for a short period but he is isolated always *with occupation*. When doing this he is reminded that everyone will be delighted to see him again when he feels better. The modern child is usually very logical and this was illustrated when I saw a child, who had been isolated in this way, open the door of the staff room. As he caught sight of the "offending" adult he said: "Are *you* feeling better now, Mrs. X?"

Another incident which was impressive in its implication was the small boy who stood watching a recently admitted child stamping his feet and shouting. When there was a break in this exhibition of bad behaviour he put his arm round his friend's shoulders and said: "You know what's the matter with you, don't you? You are DEAD SCARED."

On another occasion I saw a headmistress remove the heavy shoes from the feet of a newly admitted four-year-old boy because he was kicking the legs of the teacher. At the end of the morning session, he went to the head's room to collect his shoes. She expressed her displeasure that he should behave in such an uncontrolled way. Her surprise was as great as mine when she received the answer: "I won't do it again. I kicked because I was very frightened." Had I not heard this conversation I would have found it difficult to believe that a child of such tender years could express in words such a fundamental psychological truth.

The growth of self discipline can also be encouraged through a background of order for there can be no real freedom without order.

Some people who are considered to be progressive education-ists tend to regard training such as this as being old-fashioned and out of date. Allowing children to spend their days playing like lambs in the field, with no attempt at directing their energies or providing stimulus and progression, appears to be their idea of modern nursery "education". For them, the pendulum has swung too far in the opposite direction from the old days, when children were taught through *listening* rather than through *doing*.

Has this "modern" opinion grown as a result of the social and moral changes in this world making for so much permissiveness; so much antagonism to authority of any kind; so much readiness to take but never to give? Are they reluctant to ponder on the kind of world into which the children of today will have to live in fifteen or twenty-five years' time?

Surely a better educational policy when considering the needs of the growing children of today is to ensure that the pendulum swings in the middle so that they grow into creative and imaginative adults with disciplined minds which will enable them to support what is right and to question what is wrong.

"Absolute freedom corrupts absolutely." Remembering this, in the nursery schools which it is to be hoped will soon be available for all children : the adults concerned with them will spend *their* days saying "Isn't this fun?"

In conclusion, the twelve "rules", for parents who wish to turn their children into juvenile delinquents, drawn up by the Police Department of Houston, Texas, and circulated by them in leaflet form, strikes a strong note of warning for many parents in this country and all over the world. It is a resonant booming note in a minor key.

1. Begin at infancy to give the child everything he wants. In this way he will grow up to believe the world owes him a living.
2. When he picks up bad words, laugh at him. This will makes him think he is clever.
3. Never give him any spiritual training. Wait until he is twenty-one and let him "decide for himself".
4. Avoid the use of the word "wrong". It may develop a guilt complex. This will condition him to believe later, when he is arrested for stealing a car, that society is against him and he is being persecuted.
5. Pick up everything he leaves lying around : books, shoes,

clothes. Do everything for him so that he will be experienced in throwing all responsibility on others.

6. Let him read any printed matter he can get his hands on. Be careful that the silverware and drinking glasses are sterilized, but let his mind feast on garbage.

7. Quarrel frequently in the presence of your children. In this way they will not be too shocked when the home is broken up later.

8. Give a child all the spending money he wants. Never let him earn his own. Why should he have things as tough as you had them?

9. Satisfy his every craving for food, drink and comfort. See that every sensual desire is gratified. Denial may lead to harmful frustration.

10. Take his part against neighbours, teachers, policemen. They are all prejudiced against your child.

11. When he gets into real trouble, apologize for yourself by saying: "I never could do anything with him."

12. Prepare for a life of grief. You will be likely to have it.

THE SPIRITUAL NURTURE OF THE GROWING CHILD

Strong meat belongeth to them of full age.

Dorothy Sayers

Recently, a rural Dean in Notts said: "If some of us cared for the physical welfare of our young people as we do for their spiritual health, they would be dead. And if we cared for their mental health as for their spiritual health they would be illiterate."

The spiritual nurture of the growing child has never been so vitally important as it is today. It is not my concern to deal with *religious instruction* in schools for young people. This has been set out in the "agreed syllabus" which is a compulsory part of state education in this country whether we agree with all the recommendations or not.

For instance, some of us may feel strongly that the stories of the horror and misery of the Crucifixion and the mystery of the Resurrection are not suitable for children under seven years, and that concentration on the wonder of the renewal of life; the ritual of rebirth through the spring-time awakening is more suitable for children of this age. Such points are open to question and debate.

It is all the more important that those caring for very young children should be interested in spiritual nurture in the wider sense—the nurture of the spirit which is taking place side by side along with physical and emotional development. The nurture of this awakening spirit is the adult's greatest responsibility and our greatest privilege.

Sir Frank Mander said: "The good school has now become a social community within which children no longer *live to learn* but *learn to live*. It embodies a way of life within which the ideas of unique personality on the one hand and the community basis of society on the other is in the process of being harmonized."

It was John Ruskin who said: "To make children capable of honesty is the beginning of education", while the Duke of Wellington expressed his views in this way. "Educate without religion and you make men but clever devils."

Values are the root of all good and all evil

What we cherish and what we desire out of life in large measure makes us what we are in human character: governs our actions and their consequences.

What is ours, what is theirs?
What hurts? What helps?
How others react to our behaviour?
What is to be trusted, what feared?
What our place is in the great unknown?

Everything that lives, lives not alone or for itself and good religious education helps the divine within children to come forth and to act. For in large measure the quality of human living is learned from the values surrounding us from our earliest days. Values, of course, are first met and learned in the home. The sense of one's own value is basically taught or denied there—in the home. But values are also learned through every experience as we go through life and school plays a vital part in this.

Respect for others,
Respect for self,
Respect for learning,
Respect for good group living.

These are but a few of the values which schools *do* or *do not* foster in children. School life, especially in the earliest years in the nursery and infants' schools, helps to shape the goals, the desires and the character of people.

Even if many social and personal attitudes are fixed before

children enter a nursery school there is no need for despondency. Rather let it be remembered what Michael Angelo was heard muttering to himself as he stood before a block of marble: "Within you lies both good and evil. What comes forth depends on me." We may not be able to fight darkness but we can strike a light and then the darkness vanishes.

All good nursery education is religious for through it: integrity; kindliness; sympathetic understanding; courtesy and tolerance and a joyous appreciation of all that is good and lovely become the outstanding characteristics of the children who are benefiting from this education.

In a nutshell, nursery schools help to rear children of good will for, to quote an old Chinese proverb:

> If there is righteousness in the heart
> There will be beauty in the character.
> If there is beauty in the character
> There will be harmony in the home.
> If there is harmony in the home
> There will be order in the nation.
> If there is order in the nation
> There will be peace in the world.

It is well for all adults to remember *always* that, although in every other aspect of life we may know more than children, in matters spiritual we know far less than they do. The growing child is no spiritual vacuum to be filled by adults. There is no record anywhere in the Gospels that Christ ever *taught* children. Instead, He told His followers "to become as little children". There is probably no better modern definition of what is meant by "becoming as little children" than that given by Dorothy Sayers: "Unless you can wake on your fiftieth birthday with the same forward looking excitement and interest in life that you enjoyed when you were five, you cannot see the Kingdom of God." This surely tells us that adults should carry from their childhood; carry from their homes and earliest school days: a sense of wonder and of awe. A ready trust of other people and what has been called "gallant and light hearted happiness".

In their early years children have a wonderful sense of awareness—that numinous element which makes every day an adventure and every new experience a revelation. The three-year-old boy who, when walking along a woodland path, found a dead sparrow and then enquired of his teacher: "Where has the little bird gone and left this bit?" is an example of this. Few, save poets and artists, carry this wonderful spirit of awareness into adult life and so, in thinking of this aspect of a growing child's development, we should do so in a spirit of humility. During many years of working with and for young children most of my time was spent in learning *from* them.

In a wonderful book called *The Prophet* an Arabic poet writes of children in this way.

> We may give them our love, but not our thoughts
> For they have their own thoughts.
> We may house their bodies but not their souls
> For their souls dwell in the house of tomorrow
> Which we cannot visit, not even in our dreams.
> We may strive to be like them—but seek not to make
>   them like us
> For life goes not backward nor tarries with yesterday.

Children of nursery school years have a wonderful way of saying the right thing at the right moment when their sensitivity makes them realize that a loved one is in distress. An example of this is the story of a four-year-old child whose grandfather had just died. The distress of the grandmother as she sobbed in her daughters arms and said: "There is nothing left in life for me now. I might as well die, too" stirred the four-year-old into action. Putting her arms lovingly round her grandmother she said gently but firmly: "Grandma, you must *never never* say that again. You must always remember that we all think that you make the most wonderful gravy." This had the desired effect—Grandma felt that she was useful and needed.

Children of this age have, as a general rule, a much calmer

and more philosophical attitude to death than most adults realize. A father once sought my advice concerning the best way of preparing his small daughter for the death of a much loved grandmother who was seriously ill in hospital. He and his wife had anticipated fits of hysteria on the part of the child. Their fears were groundless. When he returned home he found neighbours commiserating with his wife over the news that her mother had just died. The reaction of the four-year-old? "Did you say that Grandma has died? Well, that's lovely. She will be company for our pussy now and when *we* die we will all be with pussy."

It was Dean Inge who said "Religion is *caught* and not *taught*". Children are catching it from adults every moment of every day. The task of the nursery school teacher is to prepare the ground for the later sowing of seeds according to the wishes of parents. The quality of the harvest depends on the way in which the ground has been prepared, especially in the earliest days at school. Men cannot gather grapes from thorns or figs from thistles and it is especially important at the present time that our consciousness of this law of sowing and reaping is heightened.

How can the ground be prepared during the earliest years to ensure a good spiritual harvest later?

The environment which includes the example of adults all day and every day is the first essential for good spiritual growth. It should be an environment which provides everything of beauty which children can understand—beauty of form; beauty of colour and beauty of harmony. Sowing the seeds of beauty in the heart of every child is the duty of parent and teacher, especially if children have to be compensated for living in towns and cities.

The good nursery school teacher provides colour and daintiness in every detail of the environment in her effort to ensure this nurture of the spirit. Flowers, growing plants, nature tables, pets of varying kinds all give rise to a sense of wonder which is the beginning of all worship. No one who has eyes to see or ears to hear need be spiritually impoverished but it is so often

Dramatic Play: identifying themselves with other people

Physical Activity: development of confidence

Self Help: training in good personal habits

Development of manipulative skill while experiencing joy through creative activity

necessary in this modern world for the teacher to provide the beauty to be seen and to be heard.

In the use of creative materials, too, the growing child is learning to leap in spirit (every moment he spends in a satisfying activity he shows a single-mindedness of spirit). There is in all growing children a vital impulse—something which ever seeks to transcend itself—they want to create and create and create. So, the provision of creative materials of all kinds *every* day (not just occasionally) and the opportunity for the child to finish his creative work if he so desires, is an essential part of this aspect of education. When considering the part played by the keeping and the care of pets it is remembered that the lowly earth worms in a wormery can teach children as much as the larger animals. The feeding and watching of birds provides another opportunity for the development of this spirit of wonder.

In the good nursery school every opportunity is taken to encourage this spirit of wonder and of awe for growing children have a capacity for enjoying the immediate. To crush or hinder the growth of that apprehension is worse than stupid.

It is sometimes questioned whether religious impulses are to be seen in such young children. Those adults who have seen children guard favourite flowers, not as possessions but as things of beauty, and who have seen the look of wonder and of awe on the face of a town-bred child at his first sight of a copse carpetted with primroses have no such doubts.

Miss Margaret McMillan, the pioneer, stressed the importance of seizing such opportunities when she described children in her first nursery school (fifty years ago) watching a snow storm. "The children stood watching; watching with lax muscles in that state of reverie which we note in them every day and which is becoming to us a condition as well defined and as deserving of respect as sleep."

Beautiful things to look at and also beautiful things to listen to. Listening to music plays an important part in the nurture of the spirit—not only the simple rhymes and songs which have possibly become a little hackneyed through frequent repetition, but listening to records of beautiful music which have stood the test of time. It was Carlyle who said: "Music leads us to the edge of the Infinite and lets us gaze for a moment into that." The sight of a group of nursery school children listening to good music: listening with a quietness and stillness which is impressive suggests that they, too, are enjoying a glimpse of the Infinite.

One day a clergyman stood in his pulpit waiting for the congregation to settle comfortably in their seats before he began his sermon. While he did so a blackbird sang his beautiful song outside the nearest window. The clergyman remained silent for some minutes and when the bird's song ended he said to the congregation: "That, my friends, is the end of the sermon," and he quietly left his pulpit.

There is a similarity in the reply of a four-year-old girl in a nursery school who stood near the nature table looking into space while all her companions were occupied. The well intentioned teacher approached her and said "Cynthia, wouldn't you like to find something to do?" The child looked up into the eyes of the teacher and said in a whisper "But I *am* doing something, I'm listening to these snowdrops." Such moments of contemplation may provide for a child a religious experience which is as deep as anything experienced by an adult.

So, in the beauty, colour and order of the nursery school environment much can be done to nurture the child's spirit. His whole day is spent in a quest after truth but the answering of questions is one means only of satisfying this search. Purposeful activity is another valuable means of helping the child to answer, or partly to answer, some of his own questions but, while remembering the need for long periods of activity, the equally important need for periods of repose for the group and for the individual child must not be overlooked. A screened corner in every nursery playroom to which a child can retire, if he so wishes, provides an opportunity for him "to think the thoughts which are his but which can never be ours."

The world does not lack wonderful things. It is we who lack wonder. Respect for every child as an individual is an unwritten rule for the staff in every good nursery school. It is remembered, too, that children need love if they are to feel love for others. Some may need the occasional caress or other outward sign of affection but the love which matters is that which makes a child realize that he is loved in spite of all his shortcomings, for he is never more in need of love than when he is most difficult. Though I understand all the mysteries of nuclear physics and have not love : I am as nothing—is a wayside pulpit concept to be remembered at all times (especially when children are difficult) if their spiritual nurture is to be fostered.

Every growing child is a personality with emotions and a will which may be in need of training. He has certain unassailable rights and is a creature of infinite possibilities. Our role is not to dominate or exploit or possess but to understand and encourage. The example of adults at all times and in all situations plays an important part in nurturing this wonderful spirit. For example, we must be tolerant of his mistakes—we all make them. None of us have reached a state of perfection or we would not be in this world; and the tolerance of mistakes is a part of understanding.

This point was once emphasized at a meeting of 200 people in an East End nursery school, but it carried no conviction. I asked a father who was a porter if he had never directed a passenger to the wrong platform; a postman if he had never delivered a letter to the wrong house; an accountant if his accounts were always correct; a mother if she had never singed her husband's shirt when ironing or mislaid her purse when shopping. Then the light dawned and there was laughter as they all admitted that they, too, were capable of making mistakes during an ordinary day's routine. "We never thought of it in that way" was the general comment.

The fantasy play of nursery school children, when they identify themselves with their parents and other adults, provides the necessary warning. The following stories illustrate this in no uncertain terms.

In an under privileged area I listened to two children who were enjoying some fantasy play in the "home corner". Father, aged four and a half years, was heard to say to mother, aged three and a half years, "All right then, when you've finished that washing up, I *will* take you to the pub for a drink. But *remember this* (at this point he thumped his small fist on the table) when you get there don't you ask me for anything 'fancy' —you'll be given a glass of beer and you'll like it!"

A few days later, in a similar situation in a district where the children had a completely different social background, "Mother", aged four years, was lying on a stretcher bed pretending to be very ill. "Father", who was just a little older, strode about in a carefree way picking up books and papers and throwing them down again. When "mother" caught sight of me she lifted her head with a great effort and said: "I wonder if you would be kind enough to telephone the doctor for me? As you can see, I have the kind of husband who simply will not realize that I am ill."

Two peeps into two completely different types of homes.

Michael, a very intelligent boy of four years, was not only observant but very logical. One morning he was one of a group enjoying musical movement and dancing round the room in bare feet. Unfortunately, the young inexperienced teacher had not arranged for the piano to be placed in such a position that she could see the children as she played.

Sitting quietly in a corner I saw Michael lift his arms with a swift movement and then hit hard the boy nearest to him. The playing and the dancing continued but when I called him to have a talk about the incident the following conversation took place:

"Michael, there are a great many things in this classroom which you can choose to do but there are a few things which you cannot do and must not do. One of them is hitting other people, especially when there is no reason for it. Please do not do this again."

Michael: "And that is quite enough from you."

"I beg your pardon, Michael!"

Michael: "Well you see, it's like this, when my mummy is nattering on and nattering on at my Dad, after a bit he says to her 'and that is quite enough from you' and then *she stops.*

Now I've said it to you and *you've* stopped haven't you?"

He then skipped off happily to continue his dancing. He had put into practice what he had seen and heard at home—and it worked!

Being truthful at all times and giving simple direct answers to all questions is another "must" for the nursery school teacher. This is not always an easy role to follow, especially if the questions concern sex but it must be remembered that such questions are also part of the child's quest after truth. They are not the prurient questionings of the adolescent. For example, the child who asked me "Would you please answer two questions for me? The first is 'where did I come from?' and the second is 'why do some mothers cut the top off a boiled egg with a knife and others mothers smash the top of a boiled egg with a spoon?' " When these questions were answered he smiled and said "Thanks very much" and ran off to finish the job he had left. The answers were just two more pieces of information to add to his store of knowledge.

It is important, however, that the adult should never be afraid to admit her lack of knowledge if she is unable to answer a question. The child will respect her for this but any "bluff" or a "lie" will destroy his faith in her for ever. "I am sorry I do not know the answer to that question but if I am able to find out I will remember to tell you" never fails to justify his faith.

Obedience during the formative years, which entails a gradual progress towards self discipline when the child is expected to obey the rules which exist and to respect the needs of his contemporaries and of adults, is another aspect of spiritual growth. "The grace of God lies in courtesy" so if adults are courteous to children it is reasonable and necessary to expect courtesy from them. *Justice* in our dealings with them is important but is not always easy to achieve when the supervision of a large group makes it difficult to be aware of the way in which certain situations arise.

Loyalty which includes loyalty to parents and to colleages is vital if the nursery schools hold as sacred in the heart of its purpose the Christian conception of parenthood and the family.

Whether a mother is thought to be good, bad or indifferent, over-anxious or feckless, she is the focus of the child's life and nothing is more likely to make for lack of confidence and security in a child than the feeling, sensed by him, that all is not well between teacher and parent.

Simple worship

For those of us who feel that it is possible to "prepare the ground" through simple worship, so that children are helped towards an assurance that God is a loving and protecting God, it is important that all sentimentality should be avoided. The tendency to present God as an all seeing and ever watchful eye is dangerous, as it might instil fear, rather than love and gratitude in the heart of the child.

A boldly printed notice stating "Remember! God is watching you here, too", which I once saw in the lavatories of a State aided school for children under seven years, was unlikely to raise in their minds a picture of an understanding and compassionate God.

Well intentioned parents are sometimes guilty of this to a lesser degree. A nursery school child failed to finish his prunes and custard at dinner one Saturday. The mother meant well when she explained that millions of children in the world were hungry and that God would be angry with him and punish him for refusing to finish the meal provided. The prunes and custard were put in the larder and the mother said firmly "You will finish them tomorrow". That night the child was wakened by a terrible thunderstorm and the parents heard him race down the stairs. They found him in the larder gobbling up the prunes and custard and saying at intervals "Really, God, I've never known so much fuss over a few *prunes*". Is it fair to use the name of God as a means of producing good behaviour?

Many children have a tremendous belief in God's personal interest in them, as did the small boy who was harassed by the attitude of his older brothers and sisters when he announced during tea that he had seen a large bear walking down the road on his way back from school. They insisted that he had seen a large dog! Eventually the argument became so heated that the offender was sent off to bed with a picture book. Later, when his mother enquired if he had said his prayers and if he had remembered to ask God to forgive him for telling a lie, he replied instantly and with conviction "Yes, I told God all about it and He said 'Don't give it another thought, old chap. As a matter of fact I thought it was a bear myself.'"

The little negro boy who was seen to be muttering to himself as he made every effort to do well in a school race also felt certain that God was interested in him personally.

When a teacher asked him what he was talking about as he ran he replied "I was talking to de Lawd and I said to him 'Oh Lawd you pick 'em up and I'll put 'em down.'"

The small child who was heard to end his nightly prayer by saying "And please God, when you have attended to everybody, try to take care of yourself because if anything happens to you *we'll be sunk*", also expressed a conviction of the Creator's personal interest and understanding.

Is it a good and wise thing to insist on formal prayers for children of nursery school years? The wise and imaginative nursery school teacher realizes that praying is a new experience for many children today and much depends on the prayers chosen for them by adults. During school hours the wise teacher is more likely to leave it to individual children to express their thanks spontaneously if they so wish. The four-year-old who thanked God for brass polish because it made the door handles and the piano pedals shine; the home-sick five-year-old who, three nights after he was rushed away from home when London nursery schools were evacuated and ended his day by saying "Dear Father God, thank you for cucumbers and wellington boots, for circular saws and for the gulls which I hope are still flying up my London river", and the five-year-old who saw his first sunset at the time when he was taking an interest in figures and said "Dear Father God this is a wonderful sky—one, two, three, four, five, six, seven, eight, nine, ten. Amen" were surely on the threshold of real prayer.

This story of a Cockney costermonger is more than impressive, for he was able to explain the meaning of prayer to his four-year-old daughter with a simplicity and clarity which most adults (trained teachers included) would find difficult to emulate.

Picture two little girls chatting while they ate their dinner in an East End nursery school. They had been admitted on the previous day and were more than excited over all that the school had to offer. Between the first and second courses I heard one child say to the other "I told my mum and dad, I did. I told them about all the lovely toys we played with; I told them about the stories and about the music when we turned ourselves into all kinds of animals and people. And then I told my dad we had to go to the lavatory and wash our hands clean, then I said to my dad 'And then we had to say our prayers and we had a "lovely" dinner'. Then my dad, he said to me 'You had to say a prayer did you? Well, remember this—never forget it—it's all right to say Jesus Christ *when your 'ands are together*' he says, but *never* say Jesus Christ if *your 'ands aren't together*' he says 'because that's *swearing*', he says."

It is known to all those who have had long experience of dealing with young children that they readily accept the discipline of silence if the period is short. They are ready and anxious to join in corporate worship if it is *shared* by adults whom they love and respect. It was Evelyn Underhill who said "Without the spirit of worship no one can educate in the true sense".

For the youngest children in an educational system however, it is well to remember that religion is in the heart and not in the knee. Some parents are still in need of tactful guidance on this question of insisting on the repetition of unsuitable prayers at night. Such as the well-intentioned mother who forced her child of three years to kneel and say the prayer "Gentle Jesus" when she was overtired after an exciting birthday party at a friend's house. The exhausted child repeated a number of times (between many yawns) the first line of the prayer. Eventually she made a great effort and said "Gentle Jesus, meek and mild . . . have you any wool?" !

It is in the beauty and repose of an ordered environment; in the unselfish participation in a community; in the pleasures of music and colour; in the free and frank discussion between children and adults; in sharing and enjoying things together which is the basis of all fellowship—in every movement of every day the young child can learn the Christian virtues.

It is vital to remember too, that for children, as for adults, the most wasted day in any week is the day on which they have not laughed, for fun is part of every child's birthright.

The various aspects of spiritual nurture would not be complete without thought being given to the need or otherwise to tell Bible stories to growing children. Certain stories, and these are few, may perhaps be told in simple language because they set patterns of friendliness, graciousness and right living. Through them adults may be able to share with children part of a great and priceless heritage—a literary heritage as well as a religious one. It is more than doubtful, however, if the telling of Bible stories can be of much help if the child is missing what he needs in creative experience and in contact with Nature. It is very difficult for some city children in our mechanized civilization to understand Bible stories connected with the country and sea-shore. The stories chosen should be within the understanding of the particular age group and wherever possible they should be related to the child's own experience in every day life. It will be found that children will do this for themselves if we do not do it for them.

One child, aged four years, asked me why baby Jesus was born in a stable and when I answered "because there was no room in the Inn" he tapped his head with his forefinger and said: "Well, if Joseph had had any sense up here he would have begged a lift on a lorry to the next Inn".

Criticism of Joseph was also expressed by another nursery school child who said to me "I think Joseph is 'soppy'. He took his wife away for a holiday and she was going to have a baby and he never even troubled to 'book up'."

At Christmas time a few years ago a group of children in a Woolwich nursery school took me to the corner of their play-room to see their Christmas crib. Unfortunately, I did not know that the previous night the teacher had accidentally broken the figure of Joseph and another had been ordered to replace it. I admired the crib but then said "It is very beautiful but where is the father? Where is Joseph?" A four-year-old boy said "Ain't he there along with Mary and the baby Jesus and the shepherds and the kings?" Before he could carry out his investigation, another child put an end to any possible discussion by saying firmly: "Well, if he *isn't* there he's on night shift!"

It is important, too, as in the telling of all stories, that any unusual words or expressions should be explained beforehand. Many nursery school teachers have had to do the explaining when clergy and Sunday school teachers have used expressions which are beyond the comprehension of young children.

Celia, when at Sunday school, had been intrigued by the story of Zachius, the tax collector listening to Christ while he sat in a sycamore tree. The word "taxes" baffled her and she later asked me for an explanation. "I only know 'taxes' which people take when they are in a hurry and have lost the bus and the 'taxes' on the bedroom wall which say 'God is Love' and things like that."

Another child talking to his friend while trying to solve a puzzle said: "Ain't God wonderful? He made everything—you and me, Mums and Dads, the animals and the birds and the trees—and he did it all with his *left hand* too." When I questioned him about this, his reply was: "Every time I go to church they say that Jesus is sitting on God's right hand so he only had his left hand to do everything with, didn't he?"

Not so very long ago there was a large meeting at the Central Hall, for heads and teachers from schools dealing with all age groups. The audience listened to numbers of erudite speeches on the teaching of such subjects as science and higher mathematics. To the relief of many of us who are interested in the heart as well as the mind of the child, the Archbishop of Canterbury stood up and, in effect, he said: "This has all been very interesting but when are we going to hear something about the imagination and curiosity in children, so that they will want to stand on tip-toes to look over hedges to view new territory?"

This was a wonderful and timely reminder and if, when standing on tip-toes to look over hedges, the children are encouraged to look upwards, as well as downwards, the results would be even more encouraging.

A story is told of a young American who once found a five dollar bill in the street. From that time onwards he seldom lifted his gaze when walking. In the course of years to come he accumulated :

29,516 buttons
54,172 pins
Twelve cents
A bent back and
A measley disposition.

He seldom saw the glare of the sunlight; the blue skies; the sheen of the stars; the smiles of friends; the blossoms in the spring.

If, as well as encouraging children to "look over hedges" they are encouraged, too, to look across to the vista ahead and above to the sky : in their own inimitable way they will thank God for all that is lovely and of good report.

THE VALUE OF STORY TELLING

The need to tell stories and to listen to them is as old as the world itself, and it remains with us through life. Adults tell each other stories day after day, if only when they recount incidents which have occurred during the working day in school, shop, office or factory; or describe the theme of the latest film or play which they have seen. I wonder how many of my readers have been forced to listen, as I have, to dramatic stories exchanged by two adults as they travel in a bus or train, or when standing in a queue. How full of details such stories can be! What pictures are conjured up in the mind of the listener as one situation follows another, and what a sense of frustration can be experienced if the appropriate bus stop or railway station is reached before the climax of the story is unfolded.

Children are insatiable listeners to stories and, like adults, they also enjoy telling them. I am tempted to think that the invention of the printing press must have come as a mixed blessing to the people of that time. The printing of books, followed by the arduous task of learning to read, must have led to a real sense of deprivation for some time. Tales sung by the bards or told around the hearth were gradually lost to them. Is it not possible that many children today who learn to read easily and quickly may also lose something of the vast heritage of stories, while they read the books and comic papers of this age? Is it not possible, also, that the backward and non-readers in a class may be even more deprived if they never hear good stories because their contemporaries in a school-room are able to enter a world of fantasy through their quickly gained skill? We have a duty to remember the special needs of the backward and non-readers. As one lover of children, who is especially sympathetic to the needs of backward readers, has said: "Why should an eagle be expected to walk up a mountain in order to see the view from the top?" Why should a slow developer have to wait until he can read in order to enjoy stories? Should he be deprived of his share in our heritage when "told" stories would give him an eagle's view of the world?

To return to the children between three and five years. There are many reasons why it is important that the daily programmes for a nursery class should include a period for story-telling. Children everywhere say "Tell us a story please", and the frequency of the demand stresses the fact that stories satisfy an important need. The gentle sigh often heard as the suitable, well told story reaches its end is evidence that a longing has been satisfied so the first and most important reason for telling stories is that children love them. They bring into their lives fun and laughter as well as an opportunity to experience sorrow as well as joy; tenderness and a desire to protect the weak and unfortunate; a realization of what is right and what is wrong; what is beautiful and what is ugly.

A link of intimacy is forged between the teller and the listeners while the children of all temperaments—the shy; the difficult and aggressive; the timid and the self-conscious gain increased understanding and knowledge. In addition, the town child can be given an insight into the wonders of nature and the sea-shore; the lives of wild and farm animals; the magic of the rolling tides and the fun of the beach.

For the country child the curtains can be drawn to portray a new world of traffic signals; fast moving traffic lights; escalators; mounted policemen; fire engines and water carts; street sellers of newspapers and hot chestnuts; under ground trains and double-decker buses.

Stories add to the young child's vocabulary and develop his appreciation of words and phrases. This is important for it is well known that lack of vocabulary restricts thinking.

All these reasons for telling stories stress the first essential in the choice of stories, for it is obvious that before any story can accomplish all which has been described it must be well chosen for the age and mental development of the children.

As she prepares the environment before the school day begins, a skilled teacher ensures that all the available indoor occupations are graded, in a way which will satisfy the varying mental ages, and that they are displayed on different low shelves. Tactful guidance is then given to the individual children so that the more advanced do not choose occupations which are so simple that they become bored; and those at an earlier stage of development are not prevented from experiencing a sense of achievement because the chosen occupation is in advance of their age and ability.

Exactly the same rules apply to story-telling. Having chosen the right type of story for the particular age group, it is important to ensure that it has certain characteristics to commend it. The construction of the story must be simple and easily understood; it must contain something of the dramatic and the ending must leave the children with a sense of contentment and repose and an instinctive feeling that there is order, rhythm, love and justice in life.

I remember well an afternoon during evacuation, when an important visitor entered the playroom while forty children listened spellbound to my story about the adventures of two pigs. Not wishing to break the continuity of the story or the concentration of the children, he picked up a small chair and very quietly joined the group. For some time no notice was taken of him but as the story neared its climax the little girl sitting next to him put her hand on his knee and whispered: "Don't *get worried;* it will be all right in the end. Nothing terrible happens to the pigs." In later years this incident became one of his favourite "after dinner" stories.

What makes stories suitable for children of nursery school age? They should, without question, deal with the familiar—with people and animals and situations which they have met or are likely to meet. The growing child is very literal and he is intensely interested in real life. As yet he is not ready for fantasy and make believe stories. Unfortunately, this is a golden rule which is broken fairly regularly by television and radio programmes, specially planned for children of this age.

Why tell or show ridiculous stories of dragons or even familiar

animals dressing up as humans and indulging in human occupations, when the child's mind can be enriched by stories which
are true to life? Intelligent children are quick to make their own
criticisms of such a portrayal, as did the four-year-old who
looked long and earnestly at a "road-safety" picture of an
animal looking to the right and to the left before it walked over
the zebra crossing to fill its basket with shopping. His comment
to me was: "This is very silly, isn't it? Animals do not go
shopping. It would have been much better if they had put a
little boy like me on the pavement." "Out of the mouths . . ."
of the young modern generation!

It is true that in their own play children have a capacity for
entering the world of fantasy but it is equally true that they
have also a capacity for returning to the real world in a matter
of seconds. The following story illustrates this point:

One summer morning, when visiting a nursery school, I found
a small group of boys between the ages of three and a half and
five years co-operating on building a boat on the lawn. They
worked with vigour and ingenuity with large packing cases
and planks, and when satisfied with their efforts they arranged
themselves on the boat with the "captain" standing with
dignity in the middle of them. As I knelt on the lawn beside
them I asked them if they were going to *Southend* but I was
told firmly that they were "off" to *Australia*. I was amazed
when I asked them what they hoped to see in Australia to be
given a long list of the attractions offered by this country. At
this point the youngest child jumped overboard. To my question
"What is he doing?" I received the reply from the captain:
"Well, as it is a lovely sunny morning I expect he's off for a
good swim." A gentle reminder, that if they were on the way
to Australia, the water was probably very deep so I hoped he
was a very good swimmer, and I was admonished in this way:
"Now *do be* sensible, Mrs. Goldsworthy! The water cannot
be as deep as all that because, after all, you *are kneeling* in it."
They were enjoying a game of fantasy but they were still in
touch with the world of reality.

At the next stage of their development children can accept

and enjoy fantasy stories for they can then say: "This isn't true but it's fun." For under fives a story should be simple, with one central idea running through it. The success of a story is assured if there is a fair amount of action and if the cumulative effect, with a repetition of phrases and sounds, is introduced.

The telling of stories has a definite technique. I once saw a four-year-old child leave her own group before the story began. She joined some children in the next room, where their teacher was also planning a period for story telling. A little later the child confided to me: "I always try to come into this room for the story because the teacher always has little lights dancing in her eyes and dancing on her teeth when *she* tells it." This testimonial illustrates the first and most important point to be remembered, if the story is to be a success, i.e. that the teacher must enjoy the story herself. It is necessary that she should enjoy every situation in it and be able to live the parts played by the people or animals involved. Identifying herself with the characters is the surest way of avoiding self-consciousness.

Not only must the story be well prepared but the teller must be word perfect. Nothing spoils a story as much as hesitancy.

The correct use of the voice is another essential if a story is to succeed. The two extremes of being histrionic and over-stimulating or using a flat monotone should be avoided. If the story teller follows the rule of telling a story in the same voice which she would use in recounting an experience to her best friend, success will be more likely. It is well to remember, too, that "expression" includes the use of gesture and facial expression, whether it be a smile or a scowl which is called for.

The value of showing illustrations or pictures in the middle of a story is a debatable point. My long experience proved to me that children were distracted by such a break. Far better, surely, to place low on the walls the day before the story is to be told any illustrations which may be necessary to ensure, for instance, that reference to kangaroos or dolphins have meaning for those children who have not visited a zoo. Illustrations should be large, brightly coloured and simple in outline. They should be true to life and animals and people should be in proportion.

The arrangement of the children in preparation for a story is important. For some unknown reason it is now considered to be old fashioned to request them to sit in a circle, either on their small chairs or cross legged on the floor. The circle is a symbol of unity and in this formation they can sit comfortably, with the minimum risk of worrying each other. If the adult joins the circle she is enabled to cast her eyes round all the children as the story proceeds. In this way she can make certain that every child is interested while, at the same time, individual children are encouraged to think that the story is being told to him. The wandering attention of a child can be regained immediately if his name is included tactfully, e.g. "And what do you think the donkey did then, Ernie?" Again, if he appears to be apprehensive about what is happening or if he fails to be amused by an incident, which provokes laughter from the rest of the group, the repetition of a sentence in a different way might enlighten him.

I have yet to be convinced that the more usual plan today—whereby a group of children are huddled so closely round the teacher that they tend to sit on each other's feet or to dig each other with their elbows—has anything to commend it. It certainly is not conducive to sustained concentration and interest. The word "circle" need not mean formality. It can mean comfort. From my observation, the huddled group round the knees of the teacher is likely to cause annoyance and frustration.

Finally, it is necessary to stress that no adult need ever be short of suitable stories for children of this age. Unfortunately, some of the many expensive books of stories published today may contain a minimum which are suitable for the formative years. Stories which are charming but are too difficult can be modified as long as the essential rules for good story telling are kept well in mind. It is worth remembering that, with a little imagination and ingenuity, the true accounts of animals in the nature columns of certain newspapers and magazines can be built into fascinating stories.

Even a letter in a correspondence column can occasionally

add to the store. One of my most successful stories, which children ask to have repeated time after time, was built up from such a source. The letter, written by a mother, described the excitement of her young family while they prepared to move to another part of the country because their father had received promotion. A certain amount of disappointment and sorrow was expressed by the children when they realized suddenly that a much loved robin, which haunted their garden and window-sills, would be left behind. Their sorrow turned to joy when the men opened the furniture van outside their new home —and out flew the robin!

The gasp of excitement; the waving of arms and the rubbing of hands as this climax was reached every time the story was repeated made the time and effort involved in padding out this story with relevant details more than worth while.

Many adults, teachers and parents may be tempted to say at this point "Why go to all this trouble? Why not read the stories?" The answer is that it is doubtful if any adult can *read* stories well until she has first discovered how to *tell* them well. Occasionally, reading stories from illustrated books provides an alibi for teachers and others who will not take the necessary trouble to learn them. Young children are then deprived of the opportunity to develop their imagination in conjuring up their own pictures of incidents and the people described. When children are older there are some stories which are more suitable for reading.

In the meantime, the book corner, which is an important part of the equipment of a good nursery school or class, provides the opportunity for children to handle books and to learn to love them for their inherent value. Suitable books add to their learning experience. Looking at them, while enjoying the repose of the secluded corner: fun, beauty and drama enters their lives, and as they learn to love books and to handle them with care, a link is provided in the gradual development of their logical thinking.

THE MODERN TRENDS IN NURSERY EDUCATION

The part-time nursery school and nursery class

(The following is a modification of a report on this subject submitted by me to the Nursery School Association of Great Britain and published by them in 1964.)

In June 1952, the Minister of Education invited the London County Council to co-operate in carrying out a limited experiment in part-time nursery education, proposed by the Central Advisory Council for Education. It was then suggested that two existing nursery schools should be used for this experiment, with forty children attending in the morning for a two and a half hour session and a completely different group of forty children attending for an afternoon session of the same length. No midday meal would be served and there would be no special arrangements for an afternoon rest.

In proposing an experiment on these lines the Central Advisory Council had in mind " . . . the pressing need to make satisfactory arrangements for the care and education of a greater number of young children, whatever their home circumstances . . ." The Minister also stated that the Central Advisory Council recognized that "in present and foreseeable circumstances, it is not possible to contemplate substantial addition to the provision of nursery school accommodation".

It was decided by the L.C.C. to use the term "nursery centre" for this type of provision, in order to distinguish it from the full-time nursery school.

I had immediately an uneasy feeling that this kind of provision could, and probably would, deteriorate into a type of play group or play centre, unless the chosen heads were not only trained nursery school teachers but experienced, mature people with the aims and ideals of nursery education in the forepart of their minds. It was important, too, that assistant teachers with similar training should be in charge of separate groups. As soon as it became quite clear that these nursery centres were justifying themselves on educational grounds, the L.C.C. agreed that their names should be changed to *nursery schools*.

The experimental part-time centres—now called schools

The first to be opened, in September 1953, was in Greenwich and occupied a prefabricated building previously used by a day nursery. The other two "centres", in Peckham and Clapham respectively, were in buildings designed especially for full-time nursery education and each formed part of the ground floor of a block of flats. Both had kitchen accommodation so that conversion to full-time would be easy if the experiment proved to be unsuccessful. It is interesting and significant that the experiment proved to be so popular that the kitchens are still not equipped as such, although good use is made of this extra accommodation.

It should be noted that these experimental schools were set up in differing types of neighbourhoods: one in an industrial area and the the other two in districts where the range of family income was fairly representative of London as a whole. In the first of the centres to be opened there was for some time a constantly changing roll, as many parents found four journeys, in two and a half to three hours, time consuming. For this reason, it was decided that in the future children should be recruited from the immediate neighbourhood.

Later Expansion of part-time education

As the success of the experimental part-time nursery schools became known and their advantages, in some cases, over full-time education were anticipated, the requests for a "change-over" came from heads in all parts of London.

Waiting lists

All nursery classes and schools had long waiting lists but it was encouraging that many parents preferred part-time to full-time education for their children. There were some parents, however, who made use of a part-time nursery school until the nearest full-time school was able to offer a place.

In the early days of the experiment it was anticipated by a great many people that the afternoon session would not be successful : that children arriving after their mid-day meal would be tired and listless and unable to benefit from what the teachers had to offer. My experience, through visiting and observing in schools and classes all over London, proved that the pattern was varied and interesting. For example, on consecutive days two different heads gave me completely different opinions. The first stated that the children arriving in the afternoon showed little inclination to spend the first part of the session in play of any kind, whether creative or physical. They preferred to sit quietly and listen to stories; to sing songs or to exchange news. Towards the end of the session they were ready for any activity provided. As an adaptable person with imaginative understanding, she realized that the children were planning their own rhythm, so she adapted the procedure which is accepted generally.

The co-operation of parents in ensuring that their children have some rest in the morning is essential if the maximum benefit is to be gained from an afternoon session.

The second head asked for my help in providing extra outside equipment for the afternoon as the children arrived like "wild ponies" anxious to use up their surplus energy!

Investigation showed that the children attending the first school had spent their morning trundling around shopping centres. Those attending the second school had been forced to sit quietly in kitchens, while their mothers prepared an early lunch and packed sandwiches for their husbands, most of whom were railway employees on shift work.

Again, I have many times admired the paintings done by children and the replies to my question : "At which session were these done?" have been varied, e.g. "Oh, the children attending in the morning, of course. The afternoon children do not paint nearly so well." Or "All these paintings were by the afternoon children. They are much more interested in colour."

General assessment

In my opinion, part-time nursery education in London was justified on educational as well as other grounds.

Experience showed that such education provided a much more satisfactory pattern of home and school, as it would surely do for *some* five-year-olds in the infants' school. It is important to remember, however, that children who have attended full or part-time nursery schools or classes have already adjusted themselves to a break from the intimacy of a home atmosphere, and at the age of five years they are ready for an increase or a furtherance of the time to be spent in school. On the other hand, five-year-olds who have not attended any type of nursery school or class would probably benefit more if they first attended the infants' school for a morning session only. It is essential that we shall be alive to the possible danger of limiting the expanding experience of five-year-old nursery school children in the interests of political expediency. To provide thousands more "places" for three- to five-year-olds at the expense of five-year-olds, who are ready for the further challenge offered by a full day in an infants' school, may make good propaganda for uninitiated members of the public. In my opinion, it would be a subtle but real denial of the value of nursery education.

Returning to part-time nursery education, the argument that this arrangement provides for twice as many children in a time of shortage is justified—but such an argument has its dangers —for it is based on the opinion that half a loaf is better than none. Responsibility lies upon the teachers concerned to see that the half a loaf is of the same quality as the whole loaf.

Unless this is remembered there is still a danger that part-time schools and classes might deteriorate into happy "play groups", and the importance of trained teachers might be overlooked by many who are anxious to use any loop-hole to underestimate their importance during a child's formative years. Their removal from nursery schools and classes might be considered a legitimate means of increasing staff in infants' schools during a period of shortage.

In another chapter I have stressed the importance of play as the great psychological need of the child, but over emphasis on this aspect of nursery education, to the exclusion of the need for stimulus, challenge and progression, is to be blind and deaf to the unmistakeable pleas of the children of this modern age.

Criticism of nursery school teachers is often expressed by other educationists who are of the opinion that the training and skill of such teachers does not go beyond the "play" situation. At this critical time, when it is possible that the age range in nursery schools may extend upwards, it behoves teachers to prove that such a criticism is unfounded.

"Let the children play" is a clarion call which, if answered, will bring joy and satisfaction into the lives of thousands who are deprived of this essential outlet but let not the cry be interpreted as an excuse for limiting other necessary activities conducive to good growth.

The problems and deficiencies of part-time education expressed by critics and doubters

In the early days of the nursery school movement great importance was attached to the mid-day meal, both for its nutritional value and as a means of establishing good social habits. These were the days when the children came from homes where parents could not afford a balanced diet, and where families were so large that survival of the fittest, rather than individual social training, was the order of the day. Today, all the necessary proteins and vitamins are available and it is exceptional for these to be beyond the parents' means, as special children's allowances ease a difficult financial situation. The education of parents in helping them to spend this money wisely is perhaps a more urgent need at the present time than the provision of meals at school—except in very deprived areas.

Children, particularly "only" children, who in their own homes present behaviour problems at meal times, were those whom I thought would suffer most from the lack of contemporary companionship and example at a school meal.

The lack of a mid-day rest is another criticism made by some people but it should be remembered that it is important that mothers should be at home with their children, either in the morning or the afternoon. Once again, this calls for the education of parents towards a realization that their young children may need a rest before or after a stimulating experience. So much depends on the home and such points should be discussed fully and frankly with parents before their children are admitted.

Co-operation between parents and teachers on everything concerning the child should be the key note in these schools and classes, as in the full-time school.

The ultimate pattern of nursery education

The case for nursery education is as strong today as it has ever been, though in stating it there has been some change of emphasis. It can no longer be said, for example, that nursery schools have "as their primary object the physical and medical nurture of the debilitated child" (Nursery Schools & Nursery classes—H.M.S.O., 1936). Improvements in child health have helped to shift the emphasis towards the social, psychological and educational needs of young children. Mental and emotional vitamins are now considered to be as important as the vitamins necessary for protection of good physical health.

This shift in emphasis means that the ultimate demand for nursery education will be greater than was envisaged in the London School Plan, as it will undoubtedly be all over the country. Not only the badly fed child or the child from over-crowded or unsuitable home conditions but the healthy, active child in a so-called luxury flat or in furnished rooms needs the opportunities for full development which good nursery education provides. More and more professional parents long for their children to share such opportunities, and the advantage to the children themselves of being a member of a cross section of society cannot be over-rated.

In a part-time nursery school where fifty per cent of the children come from a luxurious block of expensive flats and fifty per cent from the local housing estate, I once listened to two children, representative of both types of home, planning to have a tea party in the garden. This is what I heard:

First child: "Let's have a party, shall we?"

Second child: "That's a jolly good idea, I think. I will just go off to Fortnum and Mason's for some of their special savouries."

First child: "Right ho. While you're doing that I'll go down the road to Mr. Davies' shop to buy some eels and mash."

Both children walked to different parts of the garden and later returned to the garden table with plates of grass and leaves. A happy tea party followed while the meaning of savouries and eels were discussed at length.

It was interesting to observe, during my visits to this school over a long period, that the accents of the children from the poorer types of home improved while the accents of the more privileged children did not deteriorate.

Remembering all the arguments for and against part-time nursery education, I suggest that in all large towns and cities the ideal would be *a choice of full-time or part-time* within each small neighbourhood; preferably a choice between two schools or two groups within a school. This would provide an opportunity for a child to be transferred from one to the other, should the need arise.

This account would not be a fair assessment of nursery education in London as I knew it without a section devoted to the success and merits of many full-time nursery schools, where the needs of children call for more than a daily session of two and a half hours.

In the best of these schools there was no evidence, whatsoever that the children felt deprived of mother love. In no way did these schools act as a substitute for the homes. They were a complement to them.

The gradual lengthening of the day for each child made them

both full-time and part-time in a very *real* sense. The mother who co-operated in helping her child adjust himself gradually and happily strengthened the bond between parents and the staff.

Imaginative arrangements were made for the rest period, whereby only those children who were asleep remained in the horizontal until they awakened. Children who did not fall asleep after a reasonable length of time or who woke up after a short period of sleep were given occupation or allowed to get up. In this way, the one-time unobtrusive but quite definite domination of children expected to remain still and quiet after a refreshing sleep did not occur.

It would be tragic if all good full-time nursery schools and classes were forced to become part-time. The very long day which began with breakfast and ended with tea is now, fortunately, a memory of the long distant past. The modern full time nursery school has a day of reasonable length. There is sufficient elasticity to allow a mother to bring her child a little later than the agreed time of opening and to fetch him a litle earlier than the agreed time of closure, if this was in the interests of child and mother.

The voices of the critics and the doubters would be quieter if all full-time nursery schools and classes were run on the basis of the many good schools known to me over a long period of time working in the London area. Moreover, it is my opinion that the critics and doubters would be much more likely to regard nursery school teachers as professional people, of as good a standing as teachers in any other branch of education, if there were a national ruling to raise the age of admittance to three years, as in London. Personally, I would find it difficult to convince anyone that a two-year-old should not be with his mother.

Personal conclusions

For many children with a satisfactory home background, part-time nursery education has advantages over a full day. For other children who are less fortunate, a day of reasonable length planned in such a way that the time spent away from home is gradually lengthened, and where the rhythmic pattern offers serenity, as well as activity and action, the full-time nursery school offers greater advantages.

In these days of prosperity and turbulence, both full-time and part-time education is needed and an appropriate balance would be wise—a balance appropriate to the social conditions of each neighbourhood.

PARENT-TEACHER CO-OPERATION

All the flowers of all the tomorrows are in the seeds of today
CHINESE PROVERB

Some years ago, as I stood at a bus stop opposite a church in S.E. London, I became interested in a small group of young mothers with their babies in prams who had stopped to watch a clergyman paste a large poster on the church notice board. As the mothers read, they giggled and then followed a heated discussion. My curiosity aroused, I crossed the road to read the cause of this unusual reaction. What I read was:

God bless the clean clinic that weighs me with care
And the nursery school teacher who tooth-combs my hair,
And all the youth movements so toil worn for me
And God bless my mother *who never sees me.*

I knew that there was no nursery school in that district but enquiries showed that a good day nursery, provided as a necessity for the benefit of unmarried mothers, widows and others who were the chief wage earners, cared for children from babyhood to five years. This was under the supervision of the Public Health Department, but other far less satisfactory provision such as unofficial "minding" places had roused the Vicar's wrath. He obviously appreciated the importance of the mother's role in the satisfactory upbringing of her child.

The clinics still weigh children with care and youth movements may still, on occasion, be toil worn in carrying out plans to interest the youth of today. However, there is no need to stress here that the picture of the nursery school teacher was grossly misrepresented.

It has been stated previously that the mother is the focus of a growing child's life. To him she is the most important person in the world. Nevertheless a good, intelligent mother should realize that at a certain age (usually about three to three and a half years) she must, to quote Dr. Zeif, "become a link between her child, his father, other children and the outside world. She must learn how to arouse in her child the feeling of confidence, equality and security in these years and so help him to take part in the ground work of social security." It is part of every child's training that, as soon as he can stand alone among his contempories, he should meet others of his own age and learn all that sharing the life of a community can teach him.

The mother has an important part to play in helping the teacher to do all this and so complete co-operation is essential. The most carefully planned dietry; the most comfortable home or the most elaborate school building; the most complete medical service are useless unless they are used with the three fold purpose of this education in mind. It was Comenius who said : "Let the first foundations of all things be thoroughly laid unless you wish the whole superstructure to totter." Remembering this need for co-operation between teachers and parents and remembering, too, what Buddha, the great prophet, said about the importance of the mother's role it is more than regrettable that after 1,900 years of Christian teaching there is still to be seen in some schools for older children this notice :

No parents beyond this door

or, as illustrated recently in a popular educational journal, a notice outside the school gates which states :

Parents are requested to leave their children at this point and not to enter the playground.

Is there anything more likely to antagonize parents? Would it not be better to hang in the doorway a notice similar to that which can be seen in many good nursery schools :

Parents—this is your school. Its success depends to a great extent upon the interest you take in it and the co-operation you give the staff.

Some readers may remember the poster used before the war by the League of Nations Union in their campaign for international co-operation. The individual pictures showed:

(a) Two donkeys tethered together, pulling in opposite directions to reach two bales of hay placed one to their right and one to their left.
(b) They tugged against each other until they were exhausted.
(c) They put their heads together to think over their problem.

Result: they moved together to enjoy one bale of hay and later moved over to the second.

It would be useful to think of the donkeys as teacher and parent. Experience has shown that each can be a little stubborn occasionally. Co-operation, whether between teacher and parent; husband and wife or business partners does not require that one should always give way to the other. Co-operation in the true sense is based always upon a mutual understanding of each others views and aims.

In order to co-operate fully, mothers must be aware of the aims of the nursery school and the views of the staff working in it. How can this best be done? In most schools, regular meetings are held in the evening when the Headmistress and other well informed speakers will enlighten parents. At such meetings, the discussions which follow the talks play an important part in reassuring parents who need re-assurance. To discover that other children present the same difficulties as her own, at various stages of development, consoles a mother who might be feeling inadequate.

It is the responsibility of parents (both mother and father) to attend such meetings when the school staff give freely and willingly of their time to run them.

There are many essential ways in which a mother can co-operate before her child is admitted to the school. It has been explained earlier that the child must be well prepared for the break from home to school, so visiting with him at regular intervals before he is admitted assists greatly in ensuring that he looks upon it as a privilege, rather than an act of abandonment, when he eventually joins the group. It is especially important, if the school is run on a full-time basis, that some of these visits should be timed to enable the child to see the nursery school children get up from their rest beds and later to watch their joyful reunion with their parents.

Chairs placed in a corner of the playroom for the use of mothers makes it possible for the 'new entrant' to spend a gradually increasing length of time at school before he remains for the whole day. A subtle way of strengthening the child's opinion, that it would be a privilege to be a fulltime member of the community, is to gently but firmly refuse his request to remain for the whole day. A remark such as: "No. I'm sorry you cannot stay for the whole day yet. If you are lucky there will be some dinner for you quite soon and then you will be able to stay for the afternoon." This is a sure way of convincing him that a greater treat is in store.

Many mothers find it more than difficult to hand over to someone else the responsibility for children who have been dependent on them for approximately three years. It is essential that such mothers follow the advice of the teacher when they are asked to leave quietly and unemotionally.

As stated earlier, if the school is run on a part-time basis it is essential that the child should not be over-tired before he arrives for an afternoon session. While observing nursery school methods and attending the lectures and discussions parents will realize that the opportunities provided are suitable for modern children—those of this day and age. A generation ago, children were expected to be seen and not heard, and many of them, so I have been told, were made to learn and recite an endless moral poem which began:

> A good little girl sat under a tree
> Sewing as long as her eyes could see
> Then she kissed her work and folded it right
> And said 'Dear work—goodnight, goodnight.

Compare this with an advertisement which appeared recently in a local paper:

Small boy is willing to exchange a large box of marbles: a bicycle tyre: a Davy Crockett hat and a large stick of rock for a broken wireless set.

Consider also the old fashioned rhyme with some of the questions put to me by nursery school children and listed in previous chapters.

Some additional ones: "Tell me all you know about juice. Now don't tell me about orange juice and lemon juice. I mean the kind of juice which makes things work—cars and aeroplanes and things like that." A frank admission that I knew nothing about the workings of various forms of transport prompted the answer: "Well you can find out, can't you?" That typifies the attitude of the modern child.

A few weeks ago I called at a local café for some coffee. After a few minutes I was joined by a small boy (whom I discovered was three and a half years-old) and his Grandmother, who ordered a coffee for herself and a large ice-cream for her grandson. As the boy picked out small pieces of ice from the cream and arranged them round the edge of the dish, he repeated quietly: "frost, frost". Then in loud resonant tones, he said: "Granny look at these! Is this the same as 'Frost on Sunday'?"

Questions: Questions—all part of the search after truth. Rudyard Kipling describes this childhood characteristic charmingly:

"I keep six honest serving men:
(They taught me all I knew)
Their names are What and Why and When
And How and Where and Who.
I send them over land and sea;
I send them East and West;
But after they have worked for me
I give them all a rest.

I let them rest from nine 'till five
For I am busy then,

As well as breakfast, lunch and tea
For they are hungry men.
But different folk have different ways:
I know a person small,
She keeps ten million serving men
Who get no rest at all.

She sends 'em abroad on her affairs
From the second she opens her eyes
One million Hows—two million Wheres
And seven million Whys."

Parents and teachers have to agree to answer all questions truthfully and simply. This rule is particularly important when the questions concern sex. It is helpful to remember that when a growing child asks for information on any aspect of sex they are not the prurient questionings of the adolescent. The questions are asked and the answers remembered by the child because they are part of his search after truth; he wants to add to his existing store of knowledge.

It is possible that few Committees would need to meet to discuss the difficulties connected with this aspect of education in Primary and Secondary Schools, had the children been given the right training during their pre-school years. The correct handling of this aspect of education at that time can influence for the rest of their lives their attitude to sex.

A lack of the right vocabulary has been found to hinder parents in their efforts to help children in this way. Co-operation between parents and teachers is essential if children are not to be confused by varying answers. An interesting result of such co-operation is that the well informed child sometimes educates other adults! A Grandmother arrived to care for a nursery school boy while his mother gave birth to a second child. On arrival, Granny settled herself comfortably on a settee and putting her arm round her grandson she said: "I am going to stay here for two weeks. I know you will be a good boy for Granny. You see, there is a STORK in Mummy's bedroom."

The boy sprang to his feet and shouted in his anxiety: "A stork in Mummy's bedroom, Granny? I hope it doesn't frighten her, I suppose you know she's PREGNANT."

The son of a friend of mine watched with interest while his mother breast fed the new baby. When his many questions about the natural provision of this most suitable food had been answered, he said solemnly: "I think it was very clever of God to arrange for milk to come out of those breasts, but I think He would have been much more clever if He had put milk in one and orange juice in the other."

A slight criticism of the Almighty was also voiced by another child who said "I cannot think why God does not arrange for every Mummy to have a little window in her tummy so that while the baby is waiting to be born it can look out and see what the world is like." My own reaction to this suggestion is that many babies in such circumstances would decide to avoid a satisfactory birth.

The direct approach of the modern child can, on occasion, be a little embarrassing for some parents even when they have had the wisdom and imagination to answer the child's questions on sex. This happened when a small daughter rushed into the house while some friends were being entertained and called out "Daddy, please come quickly—our Flossie is marrying a very funny dog in the road. If you don't do something about it, we'll get nothing for the pups."

The following list of reminders may be helpful as a summary of the ways in which they can co-operate with the teacher, so that their combined efforts will have the desired results.

In compiling this list I have well in mind the difficulties which most mothers have to face in trying to spare time from all their manifold tasks in the home to put into practice all that is recommended.

1. Give your child the affection he needs but try not to be over-indulgent.
2. Try not to be jealous of the teacher. If your child talks a great deal about Miss X, he does so because his school

life revolves around her. He cannot re-live his daily experiences without frequent mention of her but this does not mean that she has replaced you in his affections.

3. Try to encourage, rather than criticize, remembering always that a growing child is never more in need of love than when he is most difficult. If some punitive measure is considered to be necessary as a reminder withdraw material pleasures, rather than affection.

4. Try to be consistent in your treatment. To say "Yes" to a request on Monday and "No" to the same request on Tuesday is confusing to a child. If circumstances make such a change of attitude necessary, an explanation will prevent any feeling of resentment.

5. Encourage a spirit of adventure in your child but insist that the rules of safety and of health must be obeyed without question. Children are happier if they know that limitations have been set within which they can enjoy their freedom. The child's need for control is basic. There has possibly been no more unfortunate misinterpretation than the idea that untutored licence is acceptable. The line which has to be drawn between real freedom and licence is a very fine one, but it has to be drawn if children are to be acceptable to society while they are growing, and if they are to live happily and constructively in a democracy when they have reached maturity.

6. Be careful to avoid expecting standards which are too high. This places an unnecessary strain on the child.

7. If your child is absorbed in some occupation and it is necessary to terminate it give him several minutes warning before he is asked to do so. A warning of this kind given in the Nursery School avoids scenes of irritation and frustration.

8. On all occasions praise the work done rather than the doer of it, e.g. "That is a lovely picture" rather than

"You are a clever boy to paint a picture as lovely as that."

9. One of the characteristics of the growing child is his innate sense of orderliness. As far as it can be said of anyone so young, he is very conservative and likes to know that everything has its place and is in its place. Continue to encourage this attitude and, at the same time, you will save yourself some unnecessary work.

10. Avoid talking about your child in his presence. He will find this humiliating.

11. Be brave and apologize if you have made a mistake. Children expect adults to be human and they want human relationships, not perfect ones.

12. Allow the child to help you by doing small jobs while you work. This will make him feel that he is a member of the family.

13. Remember that a child is new to words and reasoning. Do your best to speak clearly—this is very important. On one occasion, I was with a Headmistress when a local official telephoned her to ask her to arrange for a boy of six to be given free meals at school as his father had been sent to prison. We met Jimmy just as I was about to leave, so the Head asked him to tell his teacher that he was to have free dinners. Jimmy looked at her seriously and said: "I fink I could eat two but I don't fink I could eat free."

14. Remember that at all times your child is watching you and his father; listening to what you say and observing your reaction, even when you think he is absorbed in some occupation.

A mother of two children, a daughter aged six years and a son of three and a half told me of some anxious moments she experienced one Saturday morning. The daughter had decided to play "Mothers and Fathers" and set out her dolls in their beds. The brother had agreed to be Dad but at the last moment changed his mind and walked away. The mother sympathized with her daughter over the expected disappointment that her plans had fallen through. She was very surprised and more than a little concerned to be hold : "Don't worry, Mummy, I'll just have to pretend that I'm *an unmarried mother*."

After a great deal of thought, the mother decided that her young daughter had overheard this expression a few weeks earlier when she and a friend discussed the difficulty of bringing up an illegitimate child without the help of a father. At the time the six-year-old appeared to be absorbed in a book. So, parents— Beware !

15. Be truthful *at all times*, not only when answering your child's questions but when you are dealing with callers. If, for instance, you ask one of your children to answer the door-bell and tell the Rent Collector or the Insurance Representative that you are not at home, you must not be surprised if at a later date . . .

16. As a busy wife and mother you may find it difficult to spare the time to listen to your child when he wishes to talk and to communicate his ideas, but try and do this as often as possible. "Listening" is one of the most valuable contributions which Mother *and Father* can make towards the growth of self-esteem and confidence. I have related already a conversation between two children on the value of a Grandmother, as a good "listener". The following description of a Grandmother by an American child is also of interest. She does not fit in with the average modern Grandmother who is usually no more than middle-aged, but her ability to "spare time" is still her chief virtue.

"A Grandmother is a lady who has no children of her own but she likes other peoples little girls. A Grandfather is a man Grandmother. He goes for walks with boys and they talk about fishing and tractors and things like that. Grandmothers don't have to do anything but *be there*. It is enough if they drive us to market and have lots of dimes ready if they take us for walks. They should go slow past slippery leaves or caterpillars: they should never say "Hurry up". Usually they are fat and wear funny underwear. They can take their teeth and gums out. Everybody should try to have a Grandmother, especially if you don't have television because *Grandmothers are the only grown ups who have time to listen."*

17. Supervise your children's choice of television and radio programmes. Pre-school children, as well as those in older age groups, can be affected, sometimes quite seriously, by violence seen on television.

    The B.B.C.'s Director of Public Affairs stated recently that "there is much concern, and rightly so, about the increasingly large part which violence seems to play in the life of society. The B.B.C. fully recognize its responsibility in this area of social concern."

    A survey is now to be taken and more than 2,000 homes will be visited. This promises well for the future but, in the meantime, watch and listen with your children and decide which programmes are "taboo", and which are acceptable. Even those programmes specially planned for the youngest children should be censored if you are anxious to co-operate with the nursery school in avoiding fantasy stories where animals dress and behave as humans.

18. If your pre-school child is one of a family do your best to share your affection and interest in what interests them. If the nursery school child is treated as "King of the Castle" this is not only bad for him, but the older children might become resentful rather than protective.

    In conclusion, it is well to remember at all times that your "under five" is not the only one in the world who can be difficult and sometimes unmanageable.

At one stage or another every normal child presents behaviour problems. For instance, a two-year-old can be difficult because his "ego" is developing. Adolescents often present difficulties because the chemistry of their bodies is changing—they may be awkward, embarrassed and generally unsure of themselves. They may try to camouflage their misery by being aggressive and haughty. If they are given understanding and sympathy; the necessary freedom with the necessary consistent discipline before we can say "Hey Presto" they have grown into normal adults, and parents and teachers have become elderly ladies and gentlemen.

Think of it in this way. No gardener blames a rose bush if it grows up to be weak and straggling. He realizes that he has, perhaps, failed to supply the rose bush with all it needed in the way of fertilizers. Perhaps this particular bush was planted where the sun could not shine on it and the cold winds had hindered its growth.

The same rules apply to children. Give them the necessary ingredients for good growth in their earliest years and the results may be surprising.

The rules may be hard to follow but there is no need to feel discouraged or harassed. What is required of all of us who have any connection with growing children, whether Mother, Father, brothers, sisters, uncles, aunts, grandparents or neighbours is:

Not the perfection of achievement but the sincerity of effort.

Parent-teacher co-operation—the teacher's attitude to parents

Much advice, as well as guidance, has been given to parents on the need for co-operation with the school but what part should the teacher play?

First, it is vital that the school holds, as sacred in the heart of its purpose, the Christian conception of parenthood and the family so that everything possible is done to strengthen the work of the family.

However good, bad, over-indulgent or feckless a mother might appear to be, if the teacher allows any scepticism, patronage or indifference to creep into her attitude during a discussion, the great value of the school as a medium of adult education will be minimized, if not destroyed completely.

To your nursery school child his parents are the most important people in the world. To observe your welcoming smile as you greet him and his Mother when they arrive; to hear you talk to his Mother or Father in tones of friendliness and approbation is the surest way of making him feel secure when he is left in your care.

The valuable part which a good nursery school can play in furthering adult education has been proved to be impressive.

Encourage Mother and/or Father to attend Parents meetings while their child is on the waiting list, remembering that it is not always possible for both to attend the same meeting. Point out to parents the value of your adult "book corner" from which they can borrow pamphlets or leaflets on various aspects of child development. An arrangement well worth emulating is that of a headmistress in S.E. London who makes available to parents books suitable for their nursery school children to enjoy at the week-end. A small "library" fee of a few pence is charged to cover the cost of replacements and every book is provided with a cellophane jacket. This plan has proved to be exceptionally valuable in that parents are educated in the choice of books most suitable for their child's stage of development: the purchase of "comics" is reduced and, most important, the child's pleasure and concentration is increased while he is at home.

The school notice board can be another means of helping mothers e.g. if a school is run on a full-time basis, a daily Menu will help them to assess the dietary needs of their children during the rest of the day.

When a parent arrives at the school to request that her child's name should be added to the "waiting list" the value of spending as much time as possible with the mother cannot be over-estimated. Through friendly, tactful conversation the following information can be gained:

(a) The child's position in the family.
(b) If there is a younger child, what is the three-year-old's attitude to him?

(c) The child/father and father/child relationship.
(d) The type of home in which they live, e.g. a flat in a large block or a house with a garden. If the former, does the child have to be restrained in the interests of keeping on good terms with neighbours living above or below them.
(e) Is the child as a general rule difficult or responsive?
(f) Has the child any particular fears, e.g. does he demand a light in his bedroom on dark evenings?
(g) Does he wet his bed?

By this time you, the headmistress, will have discovered why the mother has visited the school, and when the child is admitted the teacher can be helped towards a real understanding of his particular needs.

If the mother is pregnant it is not only advisable, but important, to win her co-operation in postponing his start at school until at least some weeks after the birth of the baby. Discussion will enable her to realize that any risk of making the three-year-old feel that he has been pushed out of the home in the interests of the new arrival must be avoided. In the meantime, your helpful advice in recommending that the child should be encouraged to look forward to the baby's birth and to realize that it will be his baby as well as his mother's, will have good, lasting results.

In the meantime, encouraging the Mother to visit the school with her child for short periods and showing your approval of the effort she is making if she does this, provides a solid basis for future co-operation.

Imagination and tolerance on the part of the school staff is needed at all times when children on the waiting list visit with their parents for varying periods and later, when after admittance the time spent at school is increased gradually.

It is necessary, on occasion, for the staff to remind themselves that mothers have other responsibilities in addition to those connected with her pre-school child, e.g. the needs of her husband and the rest of the family have to be considered;

housework; cooking; shopping; laundry and other chores demand her attention. She may be unable to remain with her child for as long as you would wish. However demanding your work as a teacher might be, it will assist the relationship with the mother if you remember that you can give your whole attention to the children.

At the other end of the scale, a mother who is obsessed by her child may have to be persuaded, gently but firmly, that it is in his interest that she should leave the school after a reasonable length of time.

The co-operation of the teacher over the question of discipline at home and at school is vital, if later criticism of the school is to be avoided. To quote a small example, something which would only occur in schools or classes where the teacher's attitude might be too permissive, a mother who encourages her family to respect the piano as a precious instrument would naturally be perturbed if her child were allowed to bang the notes on the school piano.

Again, even if the five-year-old is a potential Michael Angelo, she would not agree that he should be allowed to paint his master-piece on her sitting-room wall.

Mutual understanding; mutual respect are the key notes of good parent-teacher co-operation. Much is expected from parents, in addition to the day to day co-operation of mothers, and the willing and wonderful help given by fathers has been impressive.

Teachers, too, have their part to play in furthering this very necessary co-operation if the buds are to blossom into flowers.

SECURITY THROUGH LOVE AND UNDERSTANDING

With the passing of time and the general concentration on the many benefits and the many atrocities of the modern age the war years, and the necessary evacuation of London school-children in September 1939, have sunk into pale insignificance for some people. Not so for the teachers and their helpers who lived night and day with evacuated nursery school children. We had a dual role, for we were substitute mothers as well as teachers. We were responsible for bathing the children and settling them into bed happily after a day of great activity when they had been "learning through doing".

Each successive day began at any time after 6.30 a.m., when lusty community singing assured us that everyone was wide awake and ready to enjoy all the opportunities which their new and exciting country life might offer.

This exacting experience taught me, and hundreds more nursery school teachers, more about child development and the ways in which succeeding stages could be satisfied than we ever learned in our training colleges, and more than we learned through day time experience in the years which followed.

Although snatched away from their parents and homes without previous preparation, the children for whom I was responsible settled quickly and happily into a beautiful country mansion. Their astonishing adjustment to a completely new way of life was expedited because they felt secure in the knowledge that for a long time their parents had looked upon us as friends. They knew, instinctively, that we loved them and that we would tell them nothing but the truth. Growing children are always adaptable if they feel secure through love.

The explanation that "The King has a very big job to do

and he wants us to stay in the lovely country until he has finished his work" was accepted with an astounding faith.

We were assisted in our more than difficult task by the indescribable kindness and loving understanding of our host and hostess, then Sir William and Lady Jowitt. This is my reason for ending this book with a tribute which was written, originally, for inclusion in a life of Lord Jowitt. Unfortunately, Lady Jowitt died before this could be done but, bearing in mind the affection and gratitude which a great number of young men and women and their parents still feel for their benefactors, I consider it right and appropriate that their humanity and unerring understanding should be recorded.

"MANY SHALL COMMEND HIS UNDERSTANDING"

These are the words on Lord Jowitt's memorial at Marlborough College. His integrity and understanding in the political field as a Lord Chancellor; and his brilliance and skill as a great lawyer will be remembered by all who value such qualities. It is my privilege to be able to commend his understanding and his devotion to a very different section of the Community—a group of very young London children, who were fortunate enough to be given a home at "Budds" in Wittersham when war was declared in September 1939.

To these children, evacuated from their homes and more than baffled by the speed with which they were taken from their parents, Lord Jowitt was known as "Saint William".

From the moment my staff and I helped the children out of the coaches we were treated as guests in every sense of the word. For children, many of whom had never been given the opportunity to enjoy nature and the unspoiled countryside, the lawns and natural gardens at "Budds" opened their eyes to a new and exciting world.

The graciousness of the "Wing" which was handed over to us as a school and home provided a setting which made an indelible impression on the minds of city children who, with few exceptions, were underprivileged. On more than one occasion, Lord Jowitt was startled by the obvious appreciation of beauty expressed by those who were so young. One instance is well remembered—a four-year-old-boy was found standing in front of an almond tree which had burst into blossom overnight. There was a look of ecstasy on his face as he stammered out: "But this is magic—simply MAGIC."

Life was so exacting for the teaching staff who had to be, in addition, substitute mothers that each day was like every other day. Not so for the children, for Friday was for them a red letter day: when they said—"It's Friday today and Saint William and Lady Jowitt will be coming from London tonight," it was often necessary for one of us to verify this fact by referring to the date on the daily newspaper. The children were always right and excitement ran high as our Host and Hostess came to show them films, while the staff had a much needed rest from routine. The varied gifts which were brought from London were another source of excitement. It is impossible to describe in words a scene which was repeated on many Sunday afternoons. It had to be seen to be believed.

Saint William collected all the "toughs", as he called them. These were the four and five-year-old-boys who had an abundance of energy. They were taken to the orchard where he walked with measured pace and great dignity, his hands clasped behind his back muttering something to himself (was he preparing a speech for the following week, I wondered?). Twenty small boys walked behind him in single file; *their* hands clasped behind their backs and also muttering to themselves. At the end of an hour or so, Lord Jowitt would hand over his followers saying: "I think they are tired out now so they should sleep well tonight."

As far as it was possible for such young children to be happy away from the security of their own homes and parents this group of evacuated children were undoubtedly happy. As the weeks and months passed their eyes began to shine and they developed physically, mentally and spiritually in an impressive way. Only on one occasion was there any sign of homesickness and the ending to the following story again demonstrates Lord Jowitt's imaginative "understanding". When preparing for bed one evening, ten children, spruce in their clean pyjamas and with well brushed hair, sat in a row on their bedroom floor *wearing their outdoor shoes*. As they turned the soles upwards the children took it in turns to crawl along the row smelling them. As they did so they began to cry and chanted "Fish and Chips", "Fish and Chips". It was then realized that the village shoemaker had used fish glue in repairing their shoes. The smell of this took the minds of the children back to their London streets and the aroma emerging from the fish and chip shops. When Lord Jowitt heard of this tears flowed unashamedly and he strode off to the kitchen where he was heard to say to the housekeeper: "Fish and Chips for *everyone* tomorrow, please." Many shall commend his understanding.

It would need a volume to relate the many ways in which this gracious host and his Countess made life so ideally happy for the innocent victims of Hitler's treachery. When some of the children had outgrown their nursery school activities, a cottage in the grounds was unhesitatingly made available for a school group so that slightly more formal education could be given.

The regular visits of the Billeting Officer, to pay the appropriate sum for the number of children involved, led to further benefits for the children. The cheques were endorsed and then handed over to be spent on them. There was one memorable occasion when every child was given a scarlet mackintosh, hat and wellington boots. They were transformed into "Budds Preparatory School".

These are just a few of the many impressive ways in which so much was done to further the well being of the children, but it was the day-to-day acts of kindness and tolerance which endeared "Saint William" to his protégés. On one occasion the nursery school invited their host and hostess to a teaparty. The look of wonderment and delight on the faces of the children, when they arrived dressed in colourful ceremonial robes, was an unforgettable sight. There were cries of "They are the King and Queen."

The children's parents were also included in the overwhelming hospitality. The first Christmas brought a coach load of mothers and fathers anxious to bring their festive gifts. They had planned to eat their sandwiches while the children had their mid-day meal but they were invited to the library where a wonderful Christmas luncheon awaited them. The parents have never forgotten this—even the coach driver stood to drink the health of Lord Jowitt with tears streaming down his face.

The moment of departure was one which my staff and I dreaded, for we anticipated floods of tears as the parents left and a more than difficult night dealing with home sick children. We had forgotten that "Saint William" was also a psychologist. As the parents settled in the coach and were preparing to wave a sad goodbye he let out a frantic call for help from the children. Only "Saint William" knew how the chickens and geese had escaped from the farm. As they ran about the main drive the plea : "Children, please help me" incited a combined effort in restoring all the feathered friends to their normal quarters. By the time this had been accomplished the coach, full of crying parents, was on its way to London. The children, physically exhausted but hilarious, settled without question into their normal routine.

When France "fell" and Lord Jowitt decided that his Kent home was no longer safe for the children, a charming letter, concerning them and the happiness they could give to others, was sent to the "Times". This brought the offer of many homes in safer areas.

As we left "Budds" for Nailsworth in the Cotswolds, a page was turned which concluded a chapter in the lives of children and staff. It was a chapter which will never be forgotten. Our appreciation and indebtedness was expressed very simply in a poem handed by the children to Lord and Lady Jowitt. The verses started :

Dear Sir William and Lady Jowitt
"The Rommany" loves you
We are sure you know it.

If proof were needed that we never forget what we learn with pleasure it is exemplified in the lives of sixty or more young men and women, who are now good husbands and wives, good parents and satisfactory citizens. Their lives might have been so very different today had they not sampled, during a crucial period in their lives, that understanding for which "many shall commend him".

> See this small one
> Tip-toe on the green foothills of the years
> Views a younger world than ours
> When we go down—he'll be the tall one.

This quotation from Day Lewis is a wonderful description of the land of childhood—a private land so difficult of approach : mandated to us and wonderfully inhabited by them.

LOOKING AT LIFE—THROUGH THE EYES OF GROWING CHILDREN

In his poem "Know you what it is to be a child?" Francis Thomson wrote:

It is to be something very different from the man of today.

It is to have a spirit yet streaming from the waters of baptism;

It is to believe in love, to believe in loveliness and to believe in belief;

It is to live in a nutshell and to count yourself King of infinite space . . .

The magic world of the young child! In imagination the boy can sail the high seas; he can quell the fiercest fire or drive the fastest train; he can also climb to the top of a tower or pilot a jet or—arrayed in white coat with a miniature stethoscope around his neck—he can relieve the sufferings of patients in a hospital ward.

The girl can take on the responsibility for the upbringing of a family or be the prima ballerina in a corps de ballet. All these experiences can be enjoyed while children sit at the kitchen table or on a park bench. This is happening while blasé adults wonder what is wrong with them. They are so unnaturally quiet—so unresponsive to the adults questions or demands.

How refreshing it can be to enter into the world of a child, especially when the national or international news makes one despair or boil with indignation over the futile efforts of adults to keep the world sane.

Growing children are so completely honest; so frank; so trusting and so imaginative and yet, when occasion demands, they can be so down-to-earth and logical. They have an astounding zest for life and their avid curiosity about people, things, life and death and about God makes every day a new adventure and every new experience a revelation. When they wake up (usually at an hour which is much too early for us adults) the day ahead can be full of magic for them. Occasionally, when a man now in his thirties waves to me as he passes my home on a motor-bike, I am reminded of a certain Saturday during evacuation, when I saw him jumping with excitement as he repeated: "Cor! It's Sunday tomorrow and there'll be scrambled egg for breakfast and church in the afternoon."

It was Dorothy Sayers who said: "Unless you can wake on your fiftieth birthday with the same forward-looking excitement as you did when you were five, you cannot see the Kingdom of Heaven." Children of this age have the enviable ability of being able to leave this world, sometimes for just a few seconds, to enter another world of their own making. These short periods of fantasy can sometimes be embarrassing and on occasion very annoying to a busy mother, whose mind is divided daily into a number of different compartments. The anger of one mother can be understood and excused when she found, on leaving a bus, that she had lost her purse. Her three-and-a-half-year-old son told her that she had left it on the seat. "Why didn't you tell me or pick it up for me?" she said fiercely. The boy rubbed his hands together, gave her a lovely smile and answered sweetly: "Well, Mummy, I suddenly thought that the purse might enjoy an extra bus ride all on its own."

Another mother, on boarding a bus with her twin girls of four years, found that there was no vacant seat. Two nuns beckoned the children and invited them to sit on their laps. Her destination in sight, the mother approached the nuns to thank them for their kindness, but before she could speak one of them whispered to her: "Please don't say anything; the children think that we are penguins."

The fact that the growing child is an ardent searcher after truth has been stated and elaborated earlier. His constant Why? Why not? How can that be? makes him a potential scientist. Yet, when the material world and the exacting standards of adults become burdensome, he has this wonderful capacity for refreshing himself by entering a world of fantasy—he can count himself King of infinite space. When children invite us to enter their world we should consider ourselves privileged and feel duly grateful.

The following stories illustrate this ability to work things out for themselves, and according to their own ideas.

The Headmistress of a nursery school gathered a group of the older children together to talk to them about a spastic child who was to be admitted the following day. She stressed these points:

> He will not be able to walk or talk like you do. He will certainly not be able to run or climb. We must all do our best to help him by being very kind and thoughtful. When he has been with us for a few days we must persuade him to do little things for himself. We must not do everything for him. I am sure you can be sensible about this.

The five year olds listened attentively and then one of them said: "He can't *talk*; he can't *walk*. What's the matter with him? Have all his batteries run down?"

It is noteworthy that, in an amazingly short period of time, the spastic child was making every effort to be independent and to share the pleasures of his contempories. The Headmistress and her staff refused to take any of the credit for this, stating that the children had accomplished it through friendly contact and gentle persuasion.

The parents of a very intelligent five-year-old girl were anxious for her to be accepted at the preparatory department of a local fee paying school of good report when she had to leave the nursery school. It was the custom for a psychologist to test the intelligence of prospective pupils and he visited the nursery school for this purpose. During the "test" he asked her to solve various graded problems saying "What do you think I have left out in this one?" or "Do you think this is complete?" Barbara's answers were quick and correct. Finally, the psychologist said: "Now, just one more thing. I would like you to draw me a picture of a man."

The child drew the required picture and the man was complete in every detail except that he was given only three fingers on his left hand. The psychologist was more than a little disconcerted when she turned to him and said: "Now, for a change, *you* tell *me* what you think I have left out."

At the same nursery school, another child proudly handed to her mother, when she arrived at the end of the day, this picture of a girl.

Excitedly she said: "Mummy, what do you think this girl has done?" The mother, afraid of her own thoughts, pulled herself together and said calmly: "I don't know: you had better tell me."

At this point, before I give the child's answer, I must describe the surprise of a few psychologists to whom I showed the picture saying: "What do you think?" Their opinion was that the child had probably been told far too much about sex.

Their astonishment equalled that of the mother when they heard the answer given by the child. "Well, this girl has eaten: some chocolate drops, some jelly babies, and a large stick of rock."

Adults are well advised not to jump to conclusions too quickly when they are mystified by a child's flight into a world of fantasy.

Wise and understanding adults are careful to accept and approve of a child's faith in a loving God, even if this may involve them in a certain "loss of face".

An example of this: one evening a "baby sitter" had an exhausting time trying to cope with a difficult child who refused to listen to reason. Thoroughly exasperated, she put the child to bed much earlier than usual saying: "When your Mummy and Daddy come home I shall tell them what a naughty girl you have been." Before she settled down to sleep the child picked up an imaginary telephone and dialled an imaginary number. The following conversation ensued: "Is that Heaven?" Pause "It is! Well I would like to talk to God please. Is that you God? Well, I have a lot to tell you." She then gave God a full account of the evening, describing her naughtiness and stressing the fact that she was sorry. She ended her conversation with the Almighty by informing him of the threat made by the "baby sitter" saying "And what do you think about that, God?" A long pause—then "Oh! thank you God. That is very kind of you. Goodbye." The imaginary telephone was replaced and the child turned to the "baby sitter" and said: "God has told me to tell you that there is absolutely no need for you to tell Mummy and Daddy anything about what has happened tonight."

The following stories illustrate the modern child's ability to make the best of a situation in which he or she might find herself in a position of doubt. A girl of four years, who lived high up in a tall block of flats listened enviously as two of her friends described their morning journeys to school:

"My Daddy drives me here every morning in his lovely car."

"I come on 37 bus and my Mummy always tries to get a front seat on the top of the bus so that I can see everything."

The envious child was silent for a few moments. She then shrugged her shoulders and said with an air of confidence:

"Well, *I* come to school every morning by LIFT. What do you think of that?"

Just before Christmas a few years ago, a well known politician accompanied me on a visit to a nursery school. He watched a child working away at an easel, painting a Nativity scene. She dipped her long-handled brushes into jars of coloured powder paints and worked with zest. The masterpiece finished, she then did a little scribbling at the corner of the paper. A sigh of satisfaction was the signal which told us that the creative urge had been satisfied. The visitor commented quietly: "That is a very interesting picture. Please tell me about it."

The child gave him the kind of look which the teacher and I understood perfectly—viz: "I should have thought it was all quite clear." However, she explained courteously that it was nearly Christmas and "here is the baby in the manger; there is the Mummy and there is the Daddy and there are the shepherds and the kings."

The visitor then said: "That is all very interesting but what are those scribbles?" The child looked somewhat perplexed for a moment and replied hesitatingly: "Those are meant to be angels." "Tell me what you know about angels?" was the next request. The child answered: "I don't know anything at all about angels" but she was evidently determined not to be out-witted for she added—"But if you happen to be interested in GOATS I can tell you quite a lot about *them*."

The span of childhood is so short that it is nothing short of sheer cruelty to curtail this satisfying and exciting stage. There is a warning for all of us in the remark made by a seven-year-old boy: "Grown-ups are always saying that they were children once—but you wouldn't think so, would you?"

Rousseau, one of the early educationists, put it in these words: "Teach the child to *live* rather than to avoid *death*. Life is not breath but action—the use of our senses; our faculties; our imagination—every part of ourselves which makes us conscious of our being. Life consists less in length of days than the keen sense of living.

It is surely our duty and our privilege as adults to let the growing child grow naturally. Those of us who are too anxious for him to pass too quickly on to what so many people consider to be real education, i.e. the skills of formal reading, writing and numbers, is to shut forcibly the door on his real world.

If we believe the modern prophets, mechanization is going to increase to an alarming extent in the years ahead. No child is a machine—he does not have to be humanized. If, as he grows naturally and confidently, we try and look at the world through his eyes : enjoying with him all that he sees and experiences and helping him to fulfill his human possibilities, it is unlikely that he will be fascinated by machines to the point of forgetting that whenever they move they do so in the direction of human well being—and not away from it.

This poem by Robert Coffin reminds us of this phase of child-hood which passes so quickly, and stresses once again the need to remember the mutual benefit to be gained from sharing the wonder, and excitement of the world.

"Little boys in Church"

Small boys in the church pews grow very fast
The first you know, those only half way up are older
And at their father's cheek or shoulder.

One day they are only bright heads that in the church light
Look as they were washed in dew
Their eyes and hair are all so new.

This Sunday only heads that dance
Next Sunday heads and coats and pants
All the boys have sprung uphill
Heads are erect and ears stand still.

One week they are boys—and then
Next week they are slim young men

Standing very still and lean
Perilously scrubbed and clean.

Enjoy each small boy while you can :
Tomorrow there will be a man
Standing taller than belief—
Little boys in church are brief.

Children are growing everywhere—not only in church.

Given the right opportunities they are growing mentally and spiritually, as well as physically. My only criticism of the poem is that the heading describes the boys as "little". Intentionally throughout this book I have referred to children as "growing children"—it would be well to cut the word "little" out of our vocabulary.

Allow them to grow for : "In as much as ye did it—or did it not."

POSTSCRIPT

Nursery schools and classes as the foundation of education as a means of rearing children good will.

Refreshment always requires a return to essentials so it would not be time wasting to be reminded of the thought provoking opinions of educationists which stress the opinions already recorded in this book. These opinions may lead you to consider the ways in which such principles can be applied in the modern world with its changing attitudes.

Professor Dewey: "I have never been able to feel much optimism regarding the possibilities of higher education when it is built on warped and weak foundations."

Professor John Vaizey (author of "Economics in Education") : "The right to a decent childhood is an absolute in a democratic and reasonably rich society. There is no conceivable justification for the intolerable start in life that we give so many."

Sir Compton MacKenzie evidently enjoyed a good start in life for he asserts : "I was happiest when I was three years old when I spent every day happily and creatively occupied."

What of the great educators of the past?

Pestalozzi stated: "We must bear in mind that the ultimate aim of education is not perfection in the accomplishments of the school but fitness for life; not the acquirement of habits of blind obedience and of prescribed diligence but a preparation for independent action. Thus education, instead of merely considering what is to be imparted to children, ought to consider first what they may be said already to possess, if not as a developed at least as an innate faculty capable of development."

Comenius stated: "Let the foundations of all things be thoroughly laid unless you want the whole superstructure to totter."

When a child leaves a good nursery school or class at the age of five years and passes on to the next stage in education what should he be like? I would say:

1. He should be a poised personality for his age and able to take his place in a group without fear or apprehension.
2. He should have established in himself good personal habits; a pride in his appearance and pride in his possessions.
3. He should be ready to co-operate with adults and to share with children.
4. He should be self-reliant and full of initiative.
5. He should have a healthy spirit of enquiry.
6. He should be able to feel and express joy through creative effort.
7. He should have developed the ability to concentrate and to see a task through to the end.
8. He should have a spiritual awareness; able to appreciate beauty and realize that there is a greater force than human force.
9. He should have learned the meaning of courtesy and the need to give as well as to take.
10. He should have developed a certain amount of tolerance.

Tolerance: This is a character trait which will be essential if the world of the future is to be peaceful and happy, with all nations, irrespective of creed, race or colour, sharing their ideas and pooling their experiences.

Adults could learn a great deal through observing the attitude of children in those nursery schools and classes where there is a percentage of coloured children. They are completely oblivious to the difference in their skins or their hair texture, or, as in some cases, the different modes of speech. They play and work together, pooling their ideas and sharing eventually the joy gained from a sense of achievement.

The following story emphasizes this point: A four-year-old girl talking to her father about her day at the nursery school ended the conversation saying "You know, Daddy, I've got a lovely special friend and we have such fun together. She came a long, long way across the sea to get here—she came from a country where the sugar grows—like the sugar we have in our tea." The father replied, "Well then, if she came from that country her face is black, isn't it?" The child pondered for a moment and then said, "Yes, I suppose it is, but I hadn't noticed."

Jo Lensford Oslo also states the problems connected with race, creed and colour and suggests a solution in the following charming poem.

Some Children Are . . .

Some children are brown
like newly baked bread;
Some children are yellow
and some are red,
Some children are white
and some almost blue
Their colours are different—
the children like you!

Some children eat porridge
and some eat figs,
Some children like ice-cream
and some roasted pigs!

Some eat raw fishes
and some Irish stew—
Their likings are different—
the children like you!

Some children say "yes"
and some say "oui"
Some say "ja"
and some say "si"
Some children say "peep"
and some say "vool"
Their words may be different
the children like you.

Some children wear sweaters
and some revozos
Some children wear furs
and some kimonos
Some children go naked
and wear only their queue
Their clothes may be different
the children like you!

Some children have houses
of stone in the streets
Some live in igloos
and some live on fleets
Some live in old straw huts
and some in new
Their houses may be different
the children like you!

Some children are Finnish
and some from Japan
Some are Norwegian
and some from Sudan
Oh yes we have children
in valley or pike

Their countries may be different—
the children alike.

Oh; if they could dance
and if they could play
altogether together
a wonderful day!
Some could come sailing
and some could just hike
So much would be different
the children alike.

It has been stated already that no nursery school however good can satisfy all the needs of growing children unless there is complete co-operation between parents and teachers so: TEACHERS AND PARENTS UNITE! Help your children to "stand on tip toes and look over the hedges to see new horizons".

Only by doing this can you ensure that they are not only enjoying the world as they know it but that they are being prepared, in an unobtrusive way to face the difficulties in their world of tomorrow.